WINNING ALEX

The Cameron Family Saga

BY SHIRLEY LARSON

The characters and events portrayed in this book are fictitious. Any similarity to persons living or dead is coincidental and not intended by the author.

Text copyright c 2015 by Shirley Larson
All rights reserved.

No part of this book may be reproduced, or stored on a retrieval system, or transmitted in any form or by any means, electronic, mechanical, photocopying, recording, or otherwise, without express written permission by the author.

Published by Shirley Larson

Chapter 1

Chapter 2

Chapter 3

Chapter 4

Chapter 5

Chapter 6

Chapter 7

Chapter 8

Chapter 9

Chapter 10

Chapter 11

Winning Alex

Chapter 1

Strange, isn't it? Just when we think we have the world by the tail, fate slaps us upside the head and we end up a light year away from where we'd been. I used to wear Michael Held dresses and Jimmy Choo shoes and hit a security code to enter my own private office. Now I dress for work in a black uniform with my yellow name tag that says Susan, don't bother with eyeshadow on my brown eyes, and put my brown hair up in a ponytail. Then I walk five blocks to spend my day behind a stainless steel counter serving coffee.

I have the morning routine down to a science. I scuff out to my kitchenette in my paint peeling-off-the-wall apartment and put the coffee on. Then I jump in the shower, pull on my work outfit, pour my pitch black coffee into a paper cup, grab a diet bar and I'm off, hiking to work in the chilly pre-dawn darkness. I cover those five blocks in a race walk. I never do it without my can of pepper spray in one gloved hand, my hot coffee in the other and my heart in my throat. As you might have guessed, the neighborhood I live in is a little…iffy.

Shirley Larson

I push through the glass doors to the shop, always with a huge sense of relief at arriving in the well-lit business tower that is in downtown Rochester, New York. I tell my boss Bob hi and don my apron. Then I begin the job of readying the shop for the day. I jockey pails of water around to dump into the big coffee urns, change the menu board if it needs to be changed, and put out the creamers, napkins and the containers with the toss away stirrers. All that stuff is routine, and by now, I can do it in my sleep. Which at four in the morning, I pretty much am.

I'm not a barista and don't plan to become one. I learned how to serve the customers from Bob. If you think it's easy to work in a coffee shop, think again. It's like any other job where you work with people.

The customers start at six thirty, trooping down from the walkway that's connected to the parking lot. They swing in through the glass door to stand in line. People used to be more impatient queuing up. Now they're on their phone or their electronic reader or into their world of social media. Makes it easier for me since they are all occupied and not shooting angry glances at me to show they think I'm the slowest server in the world. The down side to that is, they may still be on the phone when it's their turn, and they hold up one finger to you to indicate that they need to finish their conversation before they can give you their order. Because you are, after all, there to serve them. And never mind the people waiting behind them.

Most of the regulars are more savvy and easier to wait on. They know me by name of course, since I wear that name tag. I know them as decaf latte, caramel cream small, mocha Grande, well, you get the picture. It's gotten so it's a game. It started by accident when I looked up and saw this darkly handsome guy…he had to be a business exec, but he looked more like he could have been a marauding pirate in another life…and I was a little rattled because he is, well, he's good-looking and well dressed, but it's more than that. There is something about him that is just so…right. It's as if he knows there is trouble in the world and he's faced it and accepted it as part of living. I know that's crazy, but you look in those dark eyes, you know they are full of things you'd really like to talk to him about. Anyway, as I said I was rattled and I called him by his coffee choice, Yes, Mr. Regular Black? I was horribly embarrassed but he just gave me that strange smile he has, like it's an outside smile, not an inside smile. He didn't say anything, which is pretty normal for him. He can do the whole transaction without saying a word to me. The amazing part is he always leaves a five dollar tip for a three dollar cup of coffee. When I empty the tip jar, I always think fondly of Mr. Pirate Man.

Anyway, on that day of my giant faux pas, the next guy in line said, "Okay Susan, who am I?"

"You're 'make it a tall Brazilian blend cause I got a hard day ahead'." This guy, who was a suit, you know, a corporate exec like the Black Pirate, just laughed. They didn't know it but once I was like them, full of myself, thinking life was my oyster. And probably just as rude to the gal behind the coffee counter. Not anymore. What's that old saying, walk a mile in another girl's moccasins?

It got to be a shtick that I did every morning and of course Bob loved it because it brought in more customers, especially guys. But on this gloomy Thursday, the Black Pirate paid for his coffee, put his money in the tip jar and then shocked me out of my shoes by saying, "I'd like to talk to you, Susan. When do you take your break?"

"I can't say exactly," not sure I wanted to. Behind the counter, I was safe from his piratical charm. Standing anywhere close to him, his attraction was way more magnetic. "It just depends on when the rush lets up."

"Maybe around ten-thirty?" He had that look on his face of absolute assurance, as if his saying the time made it a done deal.

Oh, boy. He stood there in his charcoal gray Armani suit with that black, black hair and those blue, blue eyes and he gazed at me with that intense concentration that made me extremely nervous. Why on earth would he want to talk to me? "That's possible, but I…"

Bob came out wiping his hands on his apron. He'd been doing dishes in the back, but he has an intercom so he can hear what goes on up front.

"Mr. Cameron, you want to talk to Susan, you got her. I'll take over here."

"I don't know exactly how long we'll be," the pirate said, who I now knew was one of the Cameron brothers. Cameron, Inc. had a suite on the top floor of this building. The three Cameron men bought, renovated and sold properties all over the world and they had amassed several fortunes.

I came out from behind the counter, and, as if he had the right to do so, Mr. Cameron put a hand on my back just above the bow of my apron. I could feel that warm palm right down to my toes. He steered me out of the shop toward the elevator.

"We'll go up and talk in my office, if you don't mind."

"Would it matter if I did?" I surprised myself by sounding annoyed. I didn't like being blindsided. Since when was pirate man such good friends with Bob?

"No." He surprised me by sounding amused.

Well, at least he was honest. We stepped into the elevator and, as if he no longer had to worry about losing me, he dropped his hand and stood beside me. I swallowed a couple of times. He said office. Office was good. He was unlikely to do unspeakable things to me in his office. Mores the pity

As we ascended alone in that elevator, I stood beside him, catching whiffs of the expensive scent he wore and staring down at his expensive shoes. Most of all my mind was whirling with questions. What did the black pirate, sorry, Mr. Cameron, want with me?

After we went through the door that had Cameron, Inc. in gold letters, we ran the gauntlet past the cubicles. A guy popped his head up, another woman swiveled her desk chair around to stare at the strange sight of Alex Cameron escorting an apron-wearing coffee server to his office. The woman rolled her eyes and the guy wore a smirk. What did they think I was there for, fantasy sex? Come on, people, get real.

Winning Alex

When we went through the door that said Alex Cameron in silver letters, there was a huge secretary's desk turned at a right angle. The chair behind the desk was empty. No receptionist. We went straight through.

He said, "Have a seat" and he gestured at a maroon leather side chair with nail studs outlining the back. I had been lusting after just such a masculine chair I'd seen on line. Way out of my price range. The chair was placed in front of his desk, a wide expanse of mahogany roughly the size of the Sargasso Sea covered with neatly stacked piles of paper. A discreet upside down glance as I settled into the chair told me they were offers on property with scrawled signatures on the bottom. The room was bordered with shelves of books. I saw titles like, Property: Principles and Policies, and Understanding Property Law by John G. Sprankling, alongside The Complete Works of Shakespeare and the Critique of Pure Reason by Immanuel Kant. Rather an eclectic reader, Mr. Cameron.

"I see by that tiny frown between your brows you are wondering about my library. Are you always so observant?"

"Sorry. It's a habit I picked up. If you want to know a man, look at the books he reads. Or at least the ones he has on his shelf. The property tomes I understand.

Shakespeare, almost everybody has. Immanuel Kant, hardly anybody has."

He gave me that slight smile that acknowledged the truth of my assessment. "My father was a professor of English and philosophy. I brought a few of his books from the family home to my office. I like…having them here. I even read them on occasion."

"You must have a lot of respect for your father. Is he still teaching?"

"No. He died several years ago."

"I'm very sorry."

"Thank you." Another person wouldn't have noticed the change in his face but I did. His features grew taut with control, as if he didn't want me to see how much he still mourned the loss of his father. That alteration in his expression made me think he might be human after all.

Instead of taking his place in the chair behind the desk, he hitched up his trouser leg and perched on the desk corner. Which put him far too close to me. I suddenly went from sympathy to trepidation. I seemed to be having trouble breathing.

"Do you enjoy working in a coffee shop?"

Of all the things I expected him to say, that wasn't it. What did it matter to him whether I enjoyed my work?

I said, "Like any job, it has its good points and its bad. I enjoy seeing the people every day. I don't enjoy getting up at four in the morning. And I don't enjoy having people look down at me because I serve them coffee."

I couldn't tell whether he liked my answer or not. He just sat there studying me with those darkly blue eyes. I had a feeling that, if he wanted to, he could plumb the depths of my soul.

"Do you see yourself working there in ten years?"

Okay. I didn't know what his game was, but I'd had enough. He was so sure of himself and his ability to pry into my life. Did he expect me to sit here and expose my psyche to him while he stayed safe behind that expressionless mask of his? I stood up, which brought me eye to eye with him. "Mr. Cameron. I'm the kind of woman who doesn't answer surveys, either on the telephone or in the store. I don't enter contests because they ask too many questions. I keep my private life private. I'm not even on Facebook." I had a reason for that which I wasn't going to share with him. "My goals in life shouldn't be any concern of yours. Now if you'll excuse me…"

"Sit down, Susan." His tone was calm, but I resented it just the same. Then he said, "Please." When I eased back into the chair, he said, "I thought you understood that this is my attempt at an informal interview for a job as my assistant. What is that old saying? If you don't know what I'm doing, I must not be doing it right." His lips lifted in that half smile I was now beginning to know quite well.

His attempt at appeasing me with that lame, old-fashioned humor almost made me feel sorry for him. "Shouldn't you be giving me an application form to fill out?"

"I should," he said. "But I'm not. What did you do before you got scooped up in Bob Bleeker's net?"

I thought that was an odd way to put it. But now we were in dangerous territory. My heart sank. "I worked as an assistant-accountant."

"Why did you quit your job?"

I wanted to say I was downsized, or I didn't like the work, or I had a sick mother. But something about the way he looked at me made me feel he already knew the reason I had parted company with Kensington and Son, Inc. This wasn't a random spur of the moment interview. This was too carefully planned. He'd done his homework. Too bad he hadn't given me a chance to do mine.

I straightened in my chair a little. It was always hard to bring out the memory. "My married boss wanted me to…to have sex with him." I hated saying those words. Even though it really wasn't my fault, I felt like victims always do, that I was somehow to blame that Myer Kensington had chosen me to be his next sexual conquest. "He threatened to fire me if I didn't comply."

"Why didn't you bring a sexual harassment suit against him?"

"Another woman had already brought a suit against him and lost. I thought it was easier just to quit. But I didn't realize how vindictive he could be. He contacted several other firms where I might have found employment and told them I drank and used drugs."

"In other words, he was a total ass. You must have been furious with him.

Unwillingly, I remembered those first days after I had walked away from Kensington's. I'd felt utterly lost. I'd always seen myself as a working woman. I'd never envisioned myself as a wife with children all around. I'd always wanted a career. Now my career was gone.

"I was at first. But then I decided to leave him to the universe. And in the end, the universe took my revenge for me. His wife finally decided she'd had enough. She left him and took her money with her. The last I knew his accountant firm was floundering. I thought I'd work for

Bob at the coffee shop gig for a while and sort of…heal before I tried to jump back into the corporate world."

"And have you?" He raised one eyebrow.

"Have I what? Jumped?" His terse questions were starting to annoy me.

"Healed."

"I think so. It's all due to you, you know."

"Me?" For the first time, he looked slightly disconcerted. Good.

"You were the first customer I called by your coffee name. From there it escalated."

"Bob told me his business has tripled."

"We have been kept pretty busy but I doubt if it's because of me. It's November and the iced tea people are switching to hot coffee."

He gave me that half smile in appreciation for my attempt at modesty. "If Bob's business has picked up, it's entirely due to you…and your phenomenal memory."

"I'm not sure that's true, but if he wants to give me credit for a business surge, I'll take it."

"If you don't see yourself being a bright spot in Bob's Coffee Shop for the next several years, I wonder if you'd like to work for me."

I'd already decided I didn't want to be stuck in a cubicle doing grunt work. I probably wasn't in a position to be picky, but I had the right to at least find out what kind of job he had in mind for me. "Doing what?"

"Pretty much the same thing you did at Kensington's. You'll be my personal assistant, which will involve learning more about our property business. Since I am responsible for monies incoming and outgoing for our company, your accountant background will be very useful."

Still I hesitated. You know that old saying, if you think it's too good to be true, it usually is.

He went around to the back of his desk chair and pushed it in so he could stand behind it. Backlit as he was by the window, it was more difficult to see the expression on his face. Did he do that on purpose? Oh, yeah, I think so. His voice was smooth and calm and still had that you'd-better-listen-to-what-I-have-to-say tone. "Before you make a decision, I have to tell you that you'll be working ten hour days and sometimes longer. Your social life will be severely curtailed. Because I may need you beyond normal working hours and on an occasional weekend, your starting salary will be eighty thousand dollars."

I nearly choked. I stared at his shadowed outline thinking I must have heard incorrectly. I wanted desperately to get up out of my chair and move where I could see his face. "That's a great deal of money."

"You'll be earning it."

My bank account had taken a real hit since I'd left Kensington's. Right now, I was blowing through my savings. The money I made at the coffee shop, ninety dollars a week, didn't cover the rent I paid for my rickety apartment. I still thought there was some catch, there had to be. "I'll have to give Bob two weeks' notice."

"I've arranged everything with him. You're to start tomorrow."

"You don't waste any time, do you?"

"I deal in acquisition of property. If you see something you want, you have to act quickly."

I didn't particularly like being compared to a piece of property. But I suppose that was what I was to him, another cog in the machine of Cameron, Inc.

He said, "Do you have any questions for me?"

"Could you tell me exactly what my duties would be?"

"Your duties will be varied. You'll read contracts, check estimates on contractor work, research local properties at the courthouse, out of town properties on the internet. I may ask you to go and record deeds. At other times I'll need you to look at properties, give me your opinion on them."

"I don't know anything about buying property."

He gave me the look then, as if I were an obstinate child who was being unreasonable. "It isn't rocket science, Miss Zalinsky. It's more a matter of common sense. I'm sure you'll be up to speed in no time."

I was glad he thought so, but I wasn't all that confident. This would all be new to me. And was he going to call me by my surname now that he'd hired me? "What time would you like me to report for work?" I expected him to say eight or nine.

"We start early. I'd need you here at six-thirty."

I was a bit shocked.

"Too early? I did warn you that you'd be working long hours."

"No it's not too early. It beats my four o'clock starting time."

"Good. I'll see you tomorrow at six thirty." He came around the desk and stood looking at me for a moment. I could see his face now and he studied me with an appraisal that made me uncomfortable. "I'm assuming you do have office appropriate clothes. You should probably wear suits, or dresses with jackets. We did a little research here and discovered that, even though people deny it, they do make judgments about people based on their clothes. You are going to be the first person my clients see."

"You researched clothes?"

"It was tied in with market research we were doing. We discovered our people had better luck if they were dressed well."

So that was why he always looked like he'd been suited up by a British valet. "I'll do my best to maintain your high standards."

"Good. I have your contract ready for you to sign. Take your time and read it over if you like."

I tried to focus but all I could think of was this wonderful good fortune had fallen in my lap and I shouldn't question it. I signed quickly.

Alex took me down the hall to introduce me to his brothers. He rapped on the door with Hunter Cameron's name and ushered me in. I'd seen Hunter's picture and knew he was a heavier, more broad-shouldered version of Alex. I suppose in the absence of their father, Hunter was the patriarchal figure. Still, even at plus forty, he was drop dead gorgeous.

Hunter looked up at Alex. By the expression on his face, he was not pleased at being interrupted. "We're having a business meeting here, Alex."

It was like watching two titans coming together. Hunter's meeting was with an older woman, maybe in her forties. She wore a topaz blouse and a black skirt and ridiculously high heels. She shot a nervous look at me and clicked her purse open and shut.

"This won't take long," Alex said implacably. "I just wanted to introduce you to Susan Zalinsky, my new assistant."

"Glad to have you on the team, Miss Zalinsky. Alex has told us some great things about you. This is my client, Mrs. Rose."

I told him I was glad to meet him, but the woman was clicking her purse again. I'm not sure the brothers even heard it. But I like music and am something of a connoisseur so I have a good ear for sound.

"Hunter has just become a proud father." Alex picked up a framed picture. "He already has a photograph of his wife and daughter adorning his desk."

Grateful for the distraction, I studied the picture. I read in the paper that his wife had been a star on Broadway. It was a glamour shot, although it was hardly a case of gilding the lily. Mrs. Cameron was beautiful and their baby was stunning. How could the infant be anything else with two such beautiful parents? "That's Liz. And my daughter Madeline." His voice was filled with love and pride. "Alex is Madeline's godfather."

I looked at Alex in surprise. Somehow he didn't seem like the godfather type to me, that is, the godfather type who would spoil a little girl with a myriad of toys. He raised an eyebrow at me as if he'd read my mind.

We headed out for Justin's office and I was glad to get away from the woman's nervous purse clicking. Justin had a corner office which let in tons of light. Justin sat at his desk chair, a guitar in his hands. He played an impossibly intricate passage before setting the guitar back in its stand. I thought if that was a sample of his playing, he should be on stage, not sitting in an office.

"Wow. That was...incredible."

He grinned at me, making me like him instantly. "Just showing off for the new girl in town. Who is?"

"Susan Zalinsky." I stepped forward and held out my hand.

Winning Alex

He unfolded his long, lean body, took a step toward me and grasped my fingers in his. I could feel the callouses from constant practice on the guitar. "A brown-eyed Susan. Nice," he said, looking first at me and then at Alex. He held our joined hands up as if he were examining me. "Very nice." This was all for Alex's benefit.

"Knock it off," Alex growled, but there wasn't any real bite in his voice.

Justin laughed and released my hand. "I was only congratulating you on finding a girl who looks so…intelligent."

"You're a menace," Alex said. "Get back to work. Go play "Midnight Train to Georgia."

"How about a tune by Django Reinhardt," Justin said, an impish grin on his lips. "A little gypsy jazz to speed you on your way."

I couldn't resist saying, "Too bad Stephane Grappelli isn't here to join you."

I had Justin's complete attention now. "You are intelligent, aren't you? Don't lose this one, Alex. I like her."

"As if your opinion matters." He said it easily, as if teasing his brother was second nature. Outside in the hallway, Alex said, "Well, there. You've met the Brothers Karamazov."

"Unlike those brothers, I think you guys like each other pretty well. My guess Justin lives to tease you both but if you were in trouble, those two would close ranks."

Alex opened his office door for me to enter and I turned.

"Alex. About that woman in Hunter's office."

"What about her?"

"She seemed too…nervous. There was something…off about her. If she's selling something, I don't think I'd buy it."

He had that gleam in his eye that told me I had all his attention. "Interesting. I'll tell Hunter right away."

I left the office, wondering if it all had really been true. Had I really accepted a job at an astronomical salary? Well, astronomical for me, anyway.

I didn't sleep much that night. I kept wondering why Alex Cameron had come to me and offered me his dream job. I had a feeling I was going to be in the proverbial spot between a rock and a hard place. Alex was the stuff of a woman's dreams with that wonderfully chiseled face, black hair, dark blue eyes, and a body that must have been the product of a morning's hard work out.

And I know it sounds silly, but I thought he had a very intriguing mind. How could a woman not be attracted to him? Heaven knew I was. But that was the thing. As my boss, he was off limits. And I'd better not forget it.

I rolled over and turned out the light, thinking I'd better get some sleep. Heaven knew I'd need my wits about me if I was going to keep my equilibrium around Alex Cameron.

Chapter 2

The next morning, I drank my coffee and ate my toast and wondered if I'd been too hasty in accepting Alex's offer. What did I know about him? Yes, he was incredibly attractive and apparently enough of a family man to be godfather to his niece, but could I work with him? Maybe I should have waited and really thought about it.

Way more apprehensive than I wanted to be, I told myself it was just another day getting ready for work. I dressed carefully in a turquoise suit that I thought added color to my nondescript brown eyes and brown hair, and then stared in the mirror and tried to decide if Alex would think I looked nice.

Whoa back little pardner. No dressing for the boss. Still, he did say I should be particular about my appearance. That was the reason I took extra care with my hair and makeup, of course it was.

When I got to the high rise, Alex's office door was open. He strolled out and looked at me as if I'd been working for him for years. "Right on time, I see. Good. Come on in. I've been waiting for you. I have something to tell you." He indicated for me to sit in the same chair I'd had the other day.

"As it turns out," he said slowly, "you were right. Hunter's client came at him with a super sob story that she had this marvelous house she had to sell and she wanted him to buy it. She'd had the house appraised and she gave him a number the appraisal came in at. She wanted him to buy the house sight unseen. Turns out she didn't even own the house. She'd already signed the property over to her son. Now he was trying to sell the house out from under her. She thought if she could involve Hunter, he'd have enough power to stop her son from selling. When Hunter discovered the truth, he referred her to one of his lawyers."

"I'm sorry to hear it. It sounds like a sad case of a parent against child."

"Hunter suggested I give you a raise."

I shook my head. "No. Let me get started here first."

Alex gave me that look I was beginning to recognize as his you said the right thing look. "I told him you wouldn't take it."

"Well, you were correct. Now I need to know what my work schedule is for today."

It was heavy duty. I had contracts to read, and two properties to research, one that necessitated a trip to the courthouse. I decided I was crazy to worry about being attracted to Alex. I wouldn't have time.

It was only after I'd been at work three weeks that I discovered the reason Alex had hired me. You know how it is. You always hear the good stuff in the ladies' room. While I was in a stall, two women who worked in the cubicles and were obviously not aware of my presence stood out by the sinks and told the whole story.

"What do you think of Alex's new assistant?"

"She's a real find." The second girl's tone dripped with sarcasm. "Mousy brown hair, a suit from last year's inventory, no makeup. She even does her own nails. Marian in personnel told me that she guessed that Alex had hired this Susan babe because she'd be least likely to fall in love with him. After Jennifer, he wanted a woman who wouldn't throw herself at him at every turn. He got it with this new chickie. Her old boss sexually harassed her, so I'm sure she'll think twice before trying it on with Alex, even if he is a total stud."

There was my answer. He hadn't rejected me because of my trouble with Kensington, he'd hired me because of it. Wasn't it odd that a horrible experience had given me the best opportunity of my life?

I should have taken offense at what those women said, maybe, but instead, I was just thankful to them. Well, ladies you can talk about me all you want. For the first time in my life I'm financially secure and working for a boss who wouldn't touch me with a ten foot pole. I have a dream job.

So I sat out at that chair that had been empty when I interviewed. I quickly learned that Alex hadn't exaggerated when he said I'd be working long hours. Contracts today for the acquisition of properties are seventy to two hundred pages long. Every time the Cameron brothers bought a property, it was my job to go over the contract and make sure it said what they wanted it to say. It was a heavy duty responsibility. I often took contracts home to read, even after I'd been at the office until eight o'clock. It wasn't exactly exciting reading, either, and I had to fight the tendency to skim. I was also in charge of Alex's appointments, and I kept track of his social engagements. I was surprised to discover that he gave speeches to interested groups about property renovation. Since he invariably used slides at these talks, it was my responsibility to make sure the slides were set up so he could, with the click of a button, present them in order. The first time I did this, I screwed up. A couple of the slides were upside down. All he said to me afterwards was, next time be sure and double check them before we go in.

That first fall I was so busy trying to learn everything I needed to know that I was more or less numb. As I became more confident, I was given even more responsibility. I caught a loophole in one of the contracts, the lack of a done-by date by one of the contractors. When I pointed this out to Alex, he frowned. "One of us should have caught that. That probably saved us thousands of dollars."

At the end of the day, he said, "I know you must feel that I've given you a great deal of responsibility. You've handled it extremely well. You know what happens when a person does a good job." He smiled that smile I really didn't like, that lift of the lips that was almost as if he were following a script that said, 'boss smiles here.' "I'd like you to sit in on our acquisition meetings. This will involve some travel. It will also involve a rise in salary. How does one hundred and twenty five thousand dollars a year sound?"

"It sounds…surreal."

Winning Alex

His smile became a touch more genuine. "I take it that means you accept."

I hesitated. My social life had withered away. I only had one true blue friend left, Betsy McDougal. She and I got together when I could, sometimes on a rare Sunday afternoon when I was free. The job had taken over my life until there was nothing left. My parents seldom heard from me and they let me know they didn't like it. On the other hand, I'd moved out of my apartment into a wonderful downtown loft in a historic building that had once been a flour mill. I was thrilled that I owned the loft and it allowed me to walk to work. It was in a building that the Cameron brothers had renovated and they let me have it at a ridiculously low price. Employee discount, Alex said.

It was the typical industrial loft with exposed pipes and beams. I remember the day we toured the building. Alex had appeared in my office and told me to put my coat on, he had something he wanted me to see. He took me to this loft on the top story of a building in the mill district that had nothing in it, only bare wood floors and walls. But the ceiling held the exposed heat runs and rafters of the building. The end walls were mostly glass and they flooded the place with natural light. It was the kind of place I'd always envisioned living in, sort of raw and steeped in history. I went into ecstasies, actually forgetting that Alex was with me. I said, "The kitchen should go here with an island. This would be the main living area. Over here would be the bedroom and en suite bath."

Finally Alex said, "Susan."

"Yes?" I came back to earth.

"I brought you here so we could decide whether a woman might like a space like this. We want to build apartments that appeal to working professionals and there are a great many more women now who fit that category."

"I don't know as I'd describe myself as a typical working professional, but I love it."

"How about we sell this first apartment to you? That way, you could have the high-end finishes that suit you, quartz countertops and custom made cabinets in the kitchen and bathrooms. As for the layout, you could plan it yourself."

"You can't be serious."

It was the first time I'd ever seen her like this, thought Alex. She looks absolutely orgasmic with happiness. I thought she might not like it with its rough wood walls and exposed heat runs. Evidently, I don't know her as well as I thought I did. Her taste tallies with mine exactly. If I didn't own my condo, I'd take this place myself. Now, maybe I can finally get her out of that shit hole of an apartment in that unsafe neighborhood. If she lived here, I wouldn't have to worry about her walking home when I've kept her at work until late in the evening. She'd be two blocks from the office with fluorescent street lighting all the way.

"Would I joke about something like this?"

"No, I'm sure you wouldn't."

"Do you have enough saved for a down payment?"

"I don't know how much you'd expect for a down payment, but I have twenty thousand dollars sitting in a savings account."

"You've saved up that much?"

"When would I have time to spend it?"

His lips twitched then, in what might have been the closest thing to a genuine smile I'd seen. "Good point. Half of that is adequate for a down payment. We'll go back to the office and write it up."

"How much would it be?"

He named a price that had to be half the value of the place. "I'll take it," I said.

I was able to pick all the high-end finishes I wanted for the kitchen. I'd pretty much settled in now and I loved it, but I still had a five year mortgage with hefty monthly payments to meet. If I didn't take this promotion, would I be let go? But traveling with Alex. Could I handle that?

For that salary, I could probably travel with Godzilla.

I said yes. What was that song, something about sold my soul to the company store?

Of course, I immediately got into trouble. I started relaxing enough to finally acknowledge that I was attracted to Alex and had been right from the beginning. We were looking at pictures of property spread out over his desk and leaning there beside him, I could smell his wonderful scent. We'd spent all day together working, and I'd seen the beauty of his hands and how deft they were. And oh boy, I began to imagine what they'd feel like on my skin.

After that day, I took my so-called mousy brown hair to a hair dresser and had it cut in a style that I said I wanted because it would be easier to care for, but in actuality, I knew it would look good on me. It was one of those high fashion cuts, shorter, but long enough to curve around my cheek.

If Alex noticed my new hair style, he didn't mention it. Which was just as well. We had an unspoken pact, he and I. No being attracted to one another. No falling in bed. No sex.

Winning Alex

Our travels together were frequent. One weekend, we traveled to a Caribbean Island, St. Thomas. There in the tropical heat and the ocean breezes, I'd feel my body heat up as Alex, dressed much more informally in khaki pants and a white shirt prowled around the outside of an island house, a project the brothers were considering for purchase and renovation. He would bend over to look at the foundation and I'd think he had the nicest rear end of any man I'd ever seen. Or he'd stretch up to test a beam over a door and all his hard, clothed body would be there for me to see. Of course, I'd lie in bed at night and picture that masculine body with nothing on. Why did the man have to be so darned delectable?

On our next trip to a property in Pennsylvania, I nearly put my foot though the floor of a country shack. Alex grabbed my elbow to keep me from falling. I felt the grip of those fingers clear down to my toes. Had I seen a flare of something in his eyes? No. It was my imagination. Back home, he was the same cool, unemotional man.

On another trip to the island of St. John, we'd left a cold and wintry Rochester to tour a hotel Hunter had wanted Alex to check out. Alex thought it was a tear down. I said, "No, it could really work. It's got a quirky charm all its own."

"Like you?" he said, one eyebrow raised.

In all the time we'd worked together, he'd never made a personal remark. I was thrown. I started babbling. "It's part Victorian with a gabled roof and half Caribbean with a red façade. People would walk up to check in and think they were really in Paradise." I walked away from Alex to collect myself. "See," I said, "it's got that great little Juliet balcony."

"It's a tear down," Alex said flatly.

Still rattled by that back-handed compliment, I forgot myself. "You have absolutely no romance in your soul."

He stopped his trek through the sandy brown grass around the building and said, "What makes you think I have a soul?"

That stopped me cold. I didn't know what to say. Finally I said, "Everybody has a soul."

It was if I hadn't said a thing. He held up his camera phone and went on clicking pictures. After Alex had sent them to his brother along with the text, *Susan likes the place but I think it's a tear down,* he said, "I don't know about you, but I'm in no hurry to rush back to the cold and snow. Why don't we take some time and go to the beach?"

If he'd said, Why don't we lie down on the ground and have sex, I couldn't have been more surprised.

I said, "I don't have a swim suit."

"You could buy one," he said with that slight smile that I loved. "You should be able to afford it."

Back at the hotel gift shop, I bought a black bikini swim suit, a lacy cover up to match, a huge beach towel and a tube of sun screen. Just for fun, I added a floppy hat. When I emerged from my hotel room, Alex leaned against the wall, waiting for me. He was already in his swim suit with a white towel slung over his shoulders and sun glasses covering his eyes.

In the elevator down, I had all I could do to keep my eyes off that hard abdomen sprinkled with dark hairs and those long legs. Even his feet were beautiful, slender and well-formed. That was when I knew I had it really bad, when I started admiring his feet.

The beach was directly in front of the hotel. We walked beside each other, beach towels slung over our shoulders.

People say they go to the Caribbean for the weather and the ocean, but I think what they really go for is the sight of all the nearly naked bodies. The weather is warm, clothes are at a minimum. There are acres of bare skin everywhere you look. There's that added relief, and you'll probably think this is odd, of being in a place where it's impossible to freeze to death. The only danger from weather here is the occasional hurricane.

I spread my towel and sat down. Alex did the same, right next to me and then slid his sunglasses on over his nose. A little self-consciously, I began to apply the sun screen on my throat, arms and legs.

"Here," he said. "Roll over and let me spread some on your back."

He sounded exactly like he always did, cool and matter of fact. I told myself it was no different than as if he were Betsy, but when those masculine hands began smoothing the lotion over my bare skin, I knew there was no stretch of imagination on earth that would make me believe this was Betsy.

I could feel him undoing my bra strap and rubbing lotion all over my now completely bare back, his hands coming dangerously close to the swell on the underside of my breast. I told myself to breathe and act normal. If he didn't consider this unusual, why should I? His hands moved to the rounded part of my buttocks that were exposed below the strings of my suit. As he spread the sun screen, he pushed up on my cheeks, a move that had me instantly hot. Oh, dear heaven. Every cell in my body stung with anticipation that would never be gratified. When it seemed like he would have spread enough sunscreen in that area, he just kept massaging my rear end, most of my flesh available to him around my bikini. I wanted to protest, but again, if I did, I would be making more out of this than perhaps he intended. If I thought that was bad, his hand was now between my legs, spreading sunscreen in that intimate area of my thighs that I couldn't believe he was touching. There was only that tiny strip of material between his hand and my core. Did he know he was driving me crazy? I think he did. And I think he was doing it on purpose. With my bra strap down, I was trapped. I couldn't raise up and protest. The trouble was, I didn't want to protest. I wanted him to go right on doing what he was doing…and more.

  He rubbed both sides of that intimate area. Around the outside of my thighs and back again to that place between my legs. Just as I thought he was going to push aside the tiny strip of fabric and I would feel his fingers inside me, his hand stilled. If I knew the male libido, and I did know something about it, he was forcing himself to quit before we were past the point of no return.

I felt his hands leave me. I could hardly breathe I was so aroused. But those strong fingers were now pulling my bra strap together and fastening it.

I rolled over and said quite idiotically, "Thank you...for covering me with sunscreen."

"My pleasure," he said and there was a dark huskiness in his voice that told me he knew he'd taken advantage of me...and that I had let him.

He sat looking out at the ocean, his face totally enigmatic behind those dark mirrored glasses. But I could see that he was as aroused as I was. After a long silence, he said, "I was out of line."

"No, you weren't. I...participated."

"You have a beautiful body. But this can't happen again."

He was right, of course, but I didn't want to admit it. I wanted it to happen again. And more.

We stared out at the shining waves and the rolling surf, me still in a state of arousal and disappointment. I doubted if Alex was much better off.

We saw him at the same time, the boy who was maybe twelve years old, struggling in the surf. I thought he would be okay and climb back on his surfboard. But he didn't. He seemed to be caught. We could see him lift his head and then go under.

Now really alarmed, I stood up, trying to see him better. "He's crying for help but no one can hear him over the roar of the surf. Something's really wrong with him."

Alex leaped up and dashed through the sand and into the water. I went after him a few feet behind. Alex swam to where the boy was, not very far from shore. He quickly extracted the lad from the surf board and lifted him out of the water. The boy was coughing, which was a good sign. It meant he was able to get the water out of his throat.

It did something to me, watching Alex come out of the ocean with that boy in his arms, the surf board trailing behind. The boy's leg was twisted awkwardly. It looked as if it were broken. That was why he couldn't get back up on his board. It did something to the boy's parents too, to see Alex carrying their son. They came running. The father took the boy out of Alex's arms and the mother fell on Alex, thanking him over and over. I walked a bit away, wanting Alex to receive the parents' gratitude in private. When they departed, the boy in the arms of his father, his mother continually touching her son as if to assure herself he was there, Alex returned to me.

I said, "That was…you acted so quickly."

"Just in the right place at the right time."

I wanted to express my admiration more fully, but as always, I sensed that was not what Alex wanted. Still I blundered on. "You saved his life."

"No big deal."

"It is a big deal," I insisted. "You knew just what to do."

"Forget it." He was starting to look annoyed.

"I can't forget it. You were…wonderful." I was making him uncomfortable and I loved it. He deserved it after what he did to me, coming so near to touching me and then retreating.

"Susan, just…stop."

The devil sat on my shoulder, urging me on. "You're a super hero, Alex."

"Susan…" he warned me. He had gone from annoyed to menacing. But what was he going to do to me here on a public beach…that he hadn't already done?

I sang in my best children's playground voice, "Alex is a super hero, Alex is a super hero."

Before I knew what was happening, he scooped me up and headed out for the ocean. I knew where this was going, but I didn't care. I was actually in Alex's arms, lying against his hard abdomen. He kept going out deeper and deeper until the water splashed my butt. He was considerate enough to stop and ask, "Can you swim?"

"Yes, but I'd prefer not to do it like this..."

He opened his arms and dropped me. I went under, water up my nose, flailing my arms, trying to get my feet under me.

I came up sputtering. He'd retreated closer to the shore. I walked toward him with my most menacing face. I pushed my hair out of my eyes thinking I must look anything but beautiful at the moment.

"Sorry about your hair. Although you're the most attractive-looking drowned rat I've seen in a while..."

A drowned rat? I was more determined than ever to take my revenge. I kept walking. "How would you like to be buried in the sand?"

"Not much. I don't like sand in my ears. Sus...san. Remember I'm your boss." He backed away, his hands up. He tried to look stern, but he was smiling. Alex was actually playing with me.

"You lost all boss immunity when you dropped me in the ocean." Quick as a cat, I gripped his shoulders and shoved, intending for him to go down in the shallow water. What I didn't plan on was having him catch my shoulders and take me down with him. I also didn't intend for him to take the brunt of the fall by landing on his back and then rolling in the water, putting me under him.

We lay there in the sand staring at each other. Time seemed to stop. The ocean pulsed over us, water washing over our legs and then receding. A strand of his dark hair fell over his forehead. His eyes seemed to absorbing me, taking in every detail of my face. I could feel the cool water, the heat of the sun, the press of his chest on mine. More importantly, I could feel his erection. He couldn't know it but I had the female equivalent. I was wet and ready. More than ready.

In a tender lover's gesture, his hand cupped my cheek. "I promised myself I wouldn't cross this line," he said huskily.

"I know. I made the same promise."

"If you weren't so damn perfect…"

How blue his eyes were. And how potent he was with all his concentration centered on me. "I'm not perfect. I'm just perfect for you."

"You think so?" he said. "You don't know me."

He rolled away from me then. My body ached with disappointment. I sat up and said indignantly, "Well, that's a crock." I couldn't believe I was talking to Alex like this.

40

"I've been with you practically twenty-four seven for weeks. How could I not know you?"

"Get up," he said. "We're going home." And just like that, the lover was gone.

I stood in the hotel shower and let the lukewarm water pour over me. Whether he wanted to admit it or not, we *had* crossed the line. I thought, *I hoped,* there would be no going back. He couldn't accuse me of throwing myself at him. He'd asked for the sun screen, he'd come so close to touching me intimately that I'd darn near died, he'd rolled on top me in the surf. He wanted me as much as I wanted him. He wanted me…and he didn't want me. I have to admit, it was like dancing in the dark. I knew what he wanted…and then I didn't know. What was I going to do now? How was I going to go on working with him when all this sexual tension shimmered between us?

I got my answer. On the plane home, as we were seated in our usual spots across from each other in Cameron company private jet, he said, "Look this over."

He chucked a piece of paper across the table that separated us. It was a brief outline of the hotel we'd scoped out and it included my comments along with his. He must have put this together while he was waiting for me to pack.

This was how he was going to play it, as if that interlude on the beach had never happened. I wanted to take one of my long legs and kick him under the table. I alternated between being angry and hurt. I knew I didn't have the right, but darn it, he'd started it. My only question was…now what?

Chapter 3

I should have known. Back home it was business as usual, and I do mean business. It was, Susan I need you to look over this proposal and have it back to me in an hour. And: Alex, there's a whole page missing from this contract. And: Susan, here's the proposal for the purchase of that hotel we saw on St. John. My hotel. And: Alex, I've looked at the comps and I think the proposed purchase price is too high. And: Susan, send those comps to Hunter's and Justin's email.

At night, I lay in bed looking at my cool industrial pipes and thought I was so much worse off now than I'd been before. Before I hadn't known how wonderful Alex could be…or how sexy. Now I knew and it was killing me. I relived those moments when he was smoothing my back with sunscreen. I relived that moment when I'd seen Alex flounder slightly during his rescue and had that panic rise up in my throat for both Alex and the boy. But mostly I relived those moments in the surf when the ocean washed over me and I felt his hard body on top of mine. His hard and ready body.

I was stuck. I couldn't give up my high paying job and go back to the coffee shop just because I had a hankering for my boss and that hankering wasn't reciprocated. I had to go on being tortured day by day by day.

I celebrated Thanksgiving and Christmas with my Mom and Dad. They were full of questions about my job. I painted it in the best possible light. I told the truth, but just not the whole truth. On the day after Christmas, they came to see my loft and were quite amazed. I could tell they were relieved I had fallen on my feet.

I was glad when the holidays were over. I'd wondered what Alex was doing. I supposed he was enjoying Christmas in the bosom of his large family. A few days later, I read about Justin's marriage on Christmas Day. I was happy for him. Justin carried the burden of his health problems valiantly. I couldn't tell a lot from the picture in the newspaper, but I was sure that Anne Cameron must be quite a woman.

Back at work on Monday, I'd almost gotten used to receiving the same formal treatment from Alex, when he came out to my office on a Thursday afternoon and perched on the corner of my desk as he sometimes did.

"My goddaughter is being christened this Saturday. I wondered if you'd like to attend the service with me."

This man would never lose his ability to amaze me. He'd treated me coldly ever since the Caribbean and now he was asking me to go to an intimate family affair? "I don't know. I'm not sure I'd feel comfortable."

"Why not?" He gave me that cool, implacable look as if he didn't have the vaguest idea what I was talking about.

"I'd be a stranger attending a private family function."

"Come to the christening and then you won't be a stranger anymore."

I could tell he was in his most imperial mood. He said, "I want you to come. Will you do this for me?"

I wanted to say, am I coming as your companion or your assistant, or…what? "I suppose I could, if you want me to."

"Good," he said, slapping his knees and getting down off my desk. "I'll pick you up about ten-thirty Saturday morning. The service is at the downtown church. It will only take about twenty minutes I'm told. Then it's back to the homestead to eat. Never a Cameron family get together without food."

He disappeared back in his office, leaving me sitting there, looking down at the contract I was supposed to be studying. All the words were blurred together. In the six weeks since we were on that Caribbean beach, he'd been nothing but coldly formal. I could take his coldness. I was used to his coldness. Why didn't he stay cold? Why did he have me see-sawing back and forth like this? A boss who wanted to keep his distance from his assistant did not ask her to go with him to his goddaughter's christening.

What did one wear to a christening? I'm pretty color conscious and it seemed like black, white and red were out. I had a nice sea green dress with a draped neckline that might be appropriate. Paired with a long red wool coat and fur lined boots, I should be both stylish and warm, a difficult trick to pull off in Rochester winters.

He came for me in his red Grand Cherokee Jeep, a luxurious car that had no relationship to the army Jeeps of old. It had all the bells and whistles, a back-up camera, GPS, internal phone, leather seats that were already warm, and of course, four wheel drive. Very useful for those times when a snow storm dumped twenty inches on our fair city. Which it had done three weeks ago. Now the salt crews had been out and the snow was a mushy slush to drive through.

"Madeline was born during that last snow storm we had. Justin barely made it to the hospital on time with Liz. Hunter was out of town," Alex said. "Luckily for Justin, Anne was with them. She was Justin's girlfriend then, and now she is his wife. She's a registered nurse. She's also expecting a child."

"Your family is fortunate to have children to continue the family name. I'm sure your mother is happy."

"Happy doesn't describe our mother. Over the moon is closer. She had an episode a few years ago. It turns out she has afib. Totally treatable."

"I'm glad it wasn't anything more serious." I wanted to say…so now there's only you and Lynne left to get married, but I knew better.

The church was a historic landmark, all brick with Gothic spires. The family had gathered in a room off the sanctuary. Liz was there, bouncing the baby in her arms. Hunter watched them both and there was so much love in his eyes I could almost feel it. Justin stood with Anne, holding her hand. I liked the look of her. She was pretty, but it was more than that. She had very wise eyes and I thought she must have an old soul. Her sister Natalie stood beside Anne. She was a young teenager. Alex had told me that Natalie had leukemia, but she'd had a bone marrow transplant and was in remission. Then there was Amelia Cameron. She was seated in a chair, looking like the nobility she was. Alex took my hand and headed straight toward her. He knelt down at her side and said, "How are you feeling, Mum?"

"Oh, don't make such a fuss, Alex. How do you think I feel at the christening of my first granddaughter? I feel absolutely wonderful." She turned to me. "Alex, where are your manners? You must introduce me to this lovely young woman."

"I was just waiting until I could get a word in edgewise. This is Susan Zalinsky. She's my assistant."

Amelia extended her hand, a twinkle in her eye. "My dear girl. You have my utmost sympathy. Does he work you terribly hard?"

"Not too terribly hard, but hard enough. There's always that occasional Caribbean trip that makes up for all the hard work."

She smiled. "I'm glad you have some respite. My sons all work too hard." She said that criticism with such obvious pride.

Then it was time to enter the sanctuary. We all trooped down the aisle toward the front altar. Lynne, Alex's sister moved to walk beside me. "Because Alex is

Madeline's godfather, he'll go up front with Hunter and Liz. You can sit beside me."

"Thank you," I said. I was more than grateful for her whispered direction and her kindness. I hadn't really known what to do. She went into a front pew and I followed her.

What is it about a church sanctuary bathed in light from its stained glass windows and steeped in elemental quiet that makes one believe there must be a larger purpose to life? Two bouquets of white roses in silver vases decorated the altar table, so appropriate for this child's baptism. As the parents gathered around the baptismal font, Liz handed the baby to Alex. I could see his face from where I was sitting. I knew him so well, every expression, even though he always tried so hard to disguise any emotion he felt. At this moment, he was too moved to hide his feelings. His love for this child was written all over him. Knowing Alex, I realized how seriously he would take this responsibility of being godfather, even though both Hunter and Liz were fully capable of parenting their daughter.

The baby was dressed in a long lacy white dress which contrasted so strongly with Alex's dark suit. Liz removed the white cap from Madeline's head and the pastor put his moistened hand on her dark curls and called her by her name, Madeline Amelia Cameron. I heard a little gasp. I wondered if Amelia Cameron had known they were going to name their daughter after her.

The baby simply looked up at Alex with those dark blue eyes and didn't protest being touched by that wet hand. It was as if she knew that when Alex held her, she was safe.

The longing rose in me then, a longing so strong it was almost palpable. I wanted to see Alex holding our baby. In all my life, I don't think I ever really thought about having children. They were something far away in the misty future. My life had been all about my career and making money. But now, I felt that ache deep inside that a woman feels when she wants a child with every fiber of her being. For there was no future for me with Alex. And because of Alex, there was no future for me with anyone else.

The ceremony ended and Alex handed Madeline back to her mother. When we emerged from the church, it was snowing big, fat flakes.

The rest of the family climbed into a big limousine, but Alex caught my hand and led me to his Jeep.

When we were inside, belted and on our way out of the parking lot, I said, "That was a beautiful ceremony. Little Madeline was a perfect child. Most children cry when some stranger puts a wet hand on their head but she didn't."

"No, she didn't," he said in that cool tone of his that always seemed to discourage further conversation.

"I'm sure you'll make a wonderful godfather."

"Are you?" he said.

Why was he being such an ass? A rising anger took hold of me. Seeing him with Madeline made me realize it wasn't just sex I wanted with Alex, it was everything, a home, a baby, all of it. All of that normal life that I never thought I wanted. If I couldn't even talk to him or he to me, what was the point? "I think you should take me home now. Your family needs to celebrate without a stranger in their midst. "

"You're not a stranger."

"I want you to take me home."

We were headed up Winton toward East Avenue. He pulled the car into a side street and stopped. We sat there in the snow, the windshield wipers going back and forth.

"What's the matter? Why are you being so unreasonable?" he said, sounding as if he were the most logical person in the world.

"Me? Unreasonable? Alex, I don't know how to play this game. You want me to keep my distance, you don't want to have a personal relationship with me, yet now you bring me into the family fold. It's just too... confusing."

"What?" Finally I had aroused an emotion in him. "You think I have an answer? I see you all of my working day, and I discover it's not enough. I wanted you with me today. I needed you with me today." His hands gripped the steering wheel.

"You can't have it both ways, Alex. If you want me to keep my distance, then take me home now. If you want something else, then now is the time to show me exactly what it is you want from me."

"What do I want from you? Get out of the car."

"What?" He was going to drive off and leave me here in the snow? My anger turned into panic. Had he gone crazy?

In a low harsh tone, he said, "Get out of the car."

I suppose it was an indication of my trust in him. I didn't know what he had in mind, but I was sure he didn't intend to drive off and leave me in the cold. I opened the door and got out. He did the same and came round to me. He backed me up against the car door. "Let me show you what I want from you." With the car pressing chilly cold against my back, he cupped my head in his hands and kissed me. He seemed to be all over me, pressing down on my breasts, his legs inserted between mine. I could feel his erection against my mound.

When he lifted his head, I said, "Alex, why are we out here in the snow?"

"Because I don't want our first time to be in a car. And if we had stayed inside, it would be."

I looked up at his dark face so serious and I smiled. "What makes you think our first time won't be out in the snow?"

"Because it's too damn cold. Now will you shut up about being a stranger in my family and come home with me?" He kissed me again with a fierceness that told me Alex Cameron was a man who could feel a very strong emotion. Then he trundled me back into the car, said *shit* under his breath, a word I'd never, ever heard him use. Then he swung the car around and gunned it onto the main street

Chapter 4

It's probably not the best thing in the world to be in the bosom of your intended lover's family so aroused that you can hardly think. But I'm a healthy female animal in the prime of life and I had gone three long years without any sexual activity. To suddenly be made aware that Alex wanted me as much as I wanted him was too much stimulation for my body to take.

The dining table was laid out in a buffet, thank heaven, not a sit down dinner and the family stood about with plates of finger food, talking in little groups. Alex was on the other side of the room, deep in conversation with Justin and Hunter.

Lynne strolled up to me. "Don't mind them. It's always like this at a family gathering. They always think of some business deal they need to consult with each other about. It's pretty annoying but you'll get used to it."

"Will I?"

"Oh, yeah." She plucked an olive from her plate and popped it in her mouth. "We were all wondering what took you two so long to get here."

"We...Alex stopped the car and we had a discussion."

"Umm. Fallen for him hard, have you?"

"What makes you think that?" I thought of picking up a cheese square from my plate and eating it, but I was afraid I'd choke on it.

"The way you look at him. I'm sure I don't understand how you could fall in love with him when you work with him every day of the week and can plainly see what an ass he is."

"He's not an ass. He's just...driven."

"Well, heaven knows there won't be any surprises for you. You know each other too well."

How odd that she should say that. I felt as if I didn't know Alex at all. He kept so much of himself hidden. He had a secret he was carrying. And it was a heavy burden.

The evening ended with Alex pulling up in front of my building. I didn't know what to say or do. If he stayed parked where he was, it meant he was leaving, as there was no parking on this side of the street on Saturday.

Suddenly he swung around and parked on the other side. "This is a mistake," he growled, "but it's too late now."

I shivered, not from the cold, but from anticipation. He opened my door for me and I climbed out. The Rochester cold and wind slammed me in the face. He grabbed my hand and we ran across the street in the dark and the snow. At the door to my building, he said, "Inside, before we freeze our butts off."

He pressed the button for the old fashioned wrought iron elevator to come down and fetch us. When it arrived, he used a hand on my back to guide me inside. When the elevator began to rise, he removed his hand and stood slightly apart from me. By now, I was so confused and aroused, I didn't know what to think. I only knew that Alex was coming into my apartment. At my heavy wooden door, it only took me three tries to get the key in the lock.

"Are you nervous," he asked in that throaty voice I loved so much.

"Yes," I said.

"Me, too."

I didn't know what to make of that odd admission. Weren't men supposed to be all macho and self-confident? Alex certainly was in his business dealings. I'd seen him take down a liar at ten paces.

I'd installed coat hooks just inside the door on a wall of wood. "You can hang your coat there."

Slowly, carefully, he hung up his and then held out his hand for mine. I shrugged out of it and gave it to him. He hung it next to his. I stood there, smoothing down my dress, trying to think what I had to drink. I wasn't a beer drinker, but I did have some wine that...

"I didn't tell you how lovely you look."

"That's all right," I said, trying on a smile. "I didn't tell you how handsome you look. Would you like some coffee?"

He grabbed me and pushed me up against the wood wall. I could feel its hardness against my back. I could feel Alex's hardness against my front. "I don't want any damned coffee. And I don't think you do, either."

"No," I said, my voice husky with my own need. "I don't want any damned coffee."

He kissed me then, and I was so relieved that I opened my mouth for him even while I put my hand between us to rub his penis through the cloth of his pants.

He lifted his head. "And I thought you were shy."

I gave him a smile of pure seduction. "Maybe you don't know me as well as you think you do. "

"We should,' he said, while he slid his hand up my thigh, damn, *why did I have to wear pantyhose*, "think about this." He went all the way up to my waist and inserted his fingers under the elastic, bringing the nylon down over my hips.

"We definitely should think about this," I said, unzipping his fly and finding the access to him through his briefs, "this isn't something we should jump into."

"We're sane, reasonable people," he said. He found me and fondled my nub and it was lovely, lovely. "You know as well as I do that we should use our heads and not... Wait."

"I'm all for not waiting," I said.

"No, I mean wait. I don't have any protection. And my guess is, you're not on birth control pills."

He withdrew his hand and I let go of him. I couldn't believe this. We'd come this far and he had just now remembered he didn't have a condom? "You didn't...bring anything?"

"No. I thought I could keep this from happening." I was still in his arms and we were practically nose to nose. "Damn it, Susan. You're the best assistant I've ever had."

I stepped out of his arms and reached under my dress to yank up my pantyhose. Those darn things were almost better than a chastity belt. "I wasn't aware that having sex with a man I adore on my own time would make me any less efficient."

His face changed, and he looked slightly less tortured. That mouth, that wonderful mouth was turned up in a smile. "And do you?"

"Do I what?" I was still pulling my dress down, trying to recover some of my scattered poise.

"Adore me?" He reached out to put his hands on my shoulders but I backed away. I couldn't bear to have him touch me just now.

"You must know I do." I glared at him. "Except not so much at the moment. You really shouldn't ask a frustrated woman what she thinks of you when she's at the height of her frustration. Every man in the world walks around with a condom in his pocket. But not you. Oh, no, not you."

"I'll go to the drugstore right now."

I shook my head. "Forget it. The moment is gone. I'll go and make that coffee."

"It might be a better idea if I just…went."

I looked him straight in the eye. "That might be the best idea you've had all night."

"Ouch," he said, clutching his chest. "That one went right to the heart."

"Are you sure you have one?" I was in rare form and I wasn't about to give him any slack.

"Pretty sure. Will you kiss me goodnight?"

"I'd rather kiss a cobra."

"If I see one on the way home, I'll tell him your lips are ready."

"Alex?"

"Yes, Susan?" He looked so…Alex. So unmoved, so cool. Why didn't he feel the same frustration as I did?

"I don't care if you are my boss. In about two seconds, I'm going to throw my shoe at you."

"Goodnight, Susan. I'll see you tomorrow."

He turned to go and just for good measure, I took off my shoe and hauled it back as if I were going to throw it. He got that heavy door open in double quick time and disappeared through it.

Chapter 5

I spent the first half of the night, thinking I'd march into Alex's office Monday morning and turn in my two week notice. I spent the last half of the night worrying that Alex might fire me. In between I agonized over loving a man who was just so....weird. Because my night was such a mess, I slept the next day until one o'clock. I got up and looked out the window. Snowing again. I wasn't the kind of a girl who strapped on her snow shoes and went merrily shushing through the snow. I hated snow. I'd stay home wrapped in a cozy blanket in front of the fireplace. But I didn't want to be alone. I needed Betsy.

On the phone, she said she'd be delighted to come over and do movies and popcorn with me. The weather was that damp January cold that seeps through your skin. I knew her little Beetle was old and didn't have a good heater. "Do you want me to come and get you?" I had a Lexus I bought right after Alex had given me that gigantic raise.

Betsy was her usual cheerful self. "Don't be silly. It's only ten minutes to your place. I'll be there in a jiff."

A strong dose of Betsy was exactly what the doctor ordered.

I put on a comfy pair of lounging pajamas that had elephants marching up and down with their trunks up. An elephant with its trunk up was supposed to be good luck. I needed that luck right about now.

Betsy came in like a good wind blowing the bad air out of my loft. She stomped the snow off her boots, and shed them and her coat in my entryway. I tried to ignore looking at that wood wall and remembering the feel of it against my back and the feel of Alex's hand inside me.

We popped popcorn and made fudge, my perfect winter activities. We found an old Alan Ladd movie on TCM and settled in with a popcorn bowl and a plate of fudge laid out on my industrial coffee table.

When the movie turned to herds of cattle stampeding everywhere, Betsy, still looking at the screen, said, "Are you going to tell me what's going on now or later? Because I'm dying of suspense here."

"What makes you think anything is wrong?" Alan Ladd rode into the fray, diverting the cattle away from the upturned carriage with the little boy in it who happened to be his son in real life.

"You haven't called me in weeks."

The old man carried the little boy safely out of the way of the cattle. Thank goodness. "I haven't had time."

"So." Betsy bounced a little in anticipation. "What's going on?"

"Oh, you know. Just the usual." I kept my tone casual, as if I were talking about the weather. "Working hard, going blind reading contracts, dying to have sex with my boss."

Betsy sat up and nearly spilled popcorn all over my couch. "Are you crazy? You were just in a mess like that a few years ago."

"I know, but this is entirely different. Alex is single, he's gorgeous and he's a mystery."

"Dynamite qualities in any man."

"Besides that, I love him, and I practically told him so."

"How can you tell a man you "practically" love him?" She did that wiggle thing with her fingers to indicate quotes.

"I told him I adored him."

"What did he say to that? Sayonara, see ya around?"

"I don't remember exactly what he said. He didn't run screaming from the room, if that's what you mean.

Have you ever been dancing with someone and the lights go out? You're in complete darkness. You know the person is there, but you can't see his face. That's what it's like with Alex. I'm…dancing in the dark."

"Susan, you can't get involved with him. Look at what you have." She swept her hand around indicating my super cool loft. "I don't know what you're making, but it must be a fantastic salary."

"It is," I said ruefully.

"You didn't ask for my advice, but I'm giving it anyway. Don't go there, Suze. Don't get involved with him personally. You know how it would end. You think he'd marry you, his lowly assistant? Fat chance. He's a Cameron, babe. He's practically nobility. His mother is nobility. He's a blue blood with tons of green. When the affair is over, you're out on your keester. Lovely loft, lovely car, lovely money, gone."

"I don't think Alex would fire me…afterward."

"You think he'd want you around to remind him that he'd once gone to bed with you? No way, Hosea."

This was why I'd ask Betsy over, to give me a strong dose of her common sense. Maybe I didn't want the dose to be quite that strong.

Winning Alex

We ordered a pizza delivery and while we were biting into the wonderfully fattening food, I just realized I'd been talking about my love life and hadn't asked her a thing about hers. "So when are you getting married?"

"We haven't set a date. Sam is out of town looking for work."

"Where is he looking?"

"Some god-forsaken place in an Australian desert. An opal mine. The town is called Cobber Pedy. He's been offered a fabulous amount of money for a year's work. I'm trying to talk him out of it, but I'm afraid he's going to take it."

"You can't go half way around the world and live in a desert."

"I can, if that's what Sam wants to do."

"When will you know for sure?"

"I think in a couple of weeks. I'll keep you posted."

I reached for her over the popcorn to give her a hug. I felt so guilty that I hadn't kept in better contact with her. Now she was possibly going out of my life for a year. "I'll miss you terribly."

"No, you won't. You'll be busy with your job." She set the popcorn bowl on the table and stood up. "I have to go, Suze. Sam is going to call me around five o'clock and we're going out to dinner. Maybe I'll find out what he's planning to do then." She reached forward and hugged me. "You stay steady, Susan. You can do it."

"Not so sure about that. But I'll try."

That night I dreamed I was trying to find Betsy who'd gone wandering off in the desert. I couldn't find her. Then I saw Alex, and he was sinking into a sand dune. I woke up in a cold sweat. It was four o'clock in the morning. I got up and got a drink of water and then I lay there, thinking. Betsy was right. I had to keep my distance from Alex.

Chapter 6

I spent the whole of Monday morning being super polite and formal with Alex, discussing possible properties for purchase, current renos in progress and hiring sub-contractors in the Caribbean, all the while avoiding his eyes. At one point I had to lean over his lap top. I took extreme care not to touch him anywhere. It was so hard. I loved everything about him, his full mouth with that delicious lower lip now so familiar to me, his scent, his fine-boned hands. They all combined to put me in a state of unbearable sexual tension. My body was alive with remembering the feel of his body pressed against mine.

As for the business at hand, they had decided to go ahead with "my" hotel, which surprised me. Alex had been so strong in his objections.

At twelve-thirty I said to him, "I'm going out for lunch." Then as it had always been my custom before, I added, "Would you like your usual?"

He barely looked up from his laptop. "If you wouldn't mind."

He'd taken his cue from me and matched my formality with his own. I should have been grateful. I wasn't.

Fifteen minutes later, I laid his pastrami and Swiss cheese on whole grain bread on his desk along with his coffee. I turned to go back out of my office to eat my bagel and cream cheese when he said, "Aren't you going to eat with me?"

I put the bag with my lunch down on his desk. If this was going to be a sparring match, I wanted hands free and brain clear. "I thought you were busy."

"No, you didn't think that at all. You thought you'd escape from me by going back in your office."

I faced him squarely. There was no use delaying. The longer I put off saying what I had to say, the longer the tension would build. "I've decided you were right."

"There's a first," he said.

"Alex, I need to get through this without your asides." He swept his hand out as if to say, the floor is yours. "We need to maintain a professional relationship."

"By that you mean no sex."

"You really are the most annoying man, do you know that? You're talking about sex, right in the office, right…in front of your father's books and everything."

He raised an eyebrow. "My father's books will never tell on me. You think I'm annoying?" He sounded incredulous.

"You can be, and usually are, very formal, very polite, very non personable, never say a wrong thing. Then you come out with a statement like that."

"I thought we'd pretty much broken the ice the other night."

"I'd like to put the ice back together if we could."

"That's as impossible as it sounds…on all levels."

"I'm trying to be truthful, here, Alex."

"An effort which I applaud. It's pretty much a Cameron brothers' rule to deal in the truth. Otherwise our buildings fall down and people get hurt. The truth is, I want to have sex with you. No, make that we want to have sex with each other. Because if I've ever had a willing woman in my arms, you were it."

"Wanting doesn't necessarily mean having. It's too…risky."

"Risky for you because you might lose your job? Or risky for me because you might leave me and break my heart?"

"I'm not certain you have a heart to break."

"You think I'm heartless? I don't know what I've ever done to make you think that. Now if you could see Hunter in action, you might come to that conclusion. He hires and fires. I, on the other hand, stay in my little room and do the dull stuff. At least it seemed dull until you came along."

"I need you to be professional. Otherwise…I can't go on working for you."

"I give you twenty-four hours."

"What?" I panicked. Did he mean he was giving me one day's notice before he fired me?

"I give you twenty-four hours before you break your fine new resolution to keep your distance from me."

My panic went straight to anger, no stops along the way. "That is just…arrogant."

He sat back with those laser blue eyes trained on me. "You want truth? That's truth. And by the way, <u>Miss</u> Zalinski, you need to pack a bag tonight. We're leaving for St. John in the morning."

He went on watching me as if I were a mouse he could toy with. Hateful man. He knew darn well if he got me on that island again, I didn't stand a chance of staying away from him. "Yes, Mr. Cameron. I'll see to it, sir." I turned out to march out indignantly.

"Miss Zalinski?"

Furious, I turned around. "Yes, Mr. Cameron?"

"Your bagel and cream cheese? It's still sitting on my desk."

"Thank you very much, Mr. Cameron. You're so kind."

"Just trying to save you a trip. It's such an anticlimax to return to the scene of an argument."

He used the word anticlimax on purpose. I snatched up the brown bag and stalked out of the office. Not very assistant like behavior, I know. Was this how it was going to be? Double entendres at every turn? Surely he wouldn't stoop so low. But really that man was insufferable. And dazzling. And fun. And a great sparring partner.

Whether he was being vindictive or simply had a lot of work, he called me into his office and wordlessly, handed ten contracts for me to go over. I couldn't get through that much material in three days, let alone one afternoon.

I lugged my load out to my desk and sat down. I could get through three of them before five o'clock. I was working on contract number four when Betsy called.

"Oh, my gosh. You sound terrible," I told her.

"I feel terrible. I'm just calling to say that I have the flu and I've probably exposed you."

"That's really nice of you to think of me, but you needn't worry. I have the constitution of a horse."

"Well, I just thought you should know. It came on really quick this morning and now I feel lousy."

"Go back to bed, Bets. I'll call you tomorrow to see how you are."

I felt really bad for Betsy. I was glad she called, but I wasn't worried. I very rarely get anything and I haven't been out sick since I started working for Alex. Now I had contracts to finish.

Hunter and Justin came to collect Alex around eight o'clock for the evening meal. They greeted me as they went in to see Alex. I thought Justin gave me a rather pitying look when they left together. I'm sure he could estimate at a glance how long the work piled on my desk would take to complete.

Alex

Since this was a business meal, we Cameron brothers went to a little Italian restaurant that Hunter knew. I walked through the door, loving the smell of garlic and tomato sauce. The aroma alone would make your stomach growl. Traditional white and red table clothes covered the tables, and there were straw-wrapped wine bottles on each table to encourage diners to buy. I always found it soothing to sit here, cozy and warm on a snowy evening with a plate of spaghetti and a glass of wine.

We didn't need to order, Giuseppe knew what we wanted, three orders of spaghetti with meatballs and a loaf of crusty bread, no garlic. Hunter and Justin have been swearing off the garlic since they got married. Hunter took out his laptop and began scrolling through saleable properties. He gave us the overview first, two on the Greek Island of Cypress, two in upper New York State, a house on a lake in Missouri that looked so picturesque it should sell in five minutes, and a farm house in Iowa, of all places, one that had been built just at the end of the depression with oak cabinetry and French doors. I had to admit I wasn't giving him my full attention. I kept picturing Susan here, a napkin tucked in her neck jutting out over those lovely breasts, me forking spaghetti past her beautiful lips into her mouth. I'd bring her here if I could ever break through her reconstructed iceberg. Or better yet, I'd have her stretched out on that super big island she had in her kitchen and eat spaghetti off her naked abdomen. I'd twirl a couple of strands around her breasts. I wondered if you could get a spaghetti strand to stay entwined around a nipple. I went hard instantly.

"Alex?" Justin grabbed my arm. "You aren't with us, brother." He grinned as if he had almost read my thoughts. To distract him, I said, "How's your wife?"

"Occasionally a little green around the gills. I'm a great comfort to her. I tell her she's so nauseated because she's having twins."

"That sounds like you." It sounded like the old Justin, the fun Justin, the Justin who'd gone missing for almost a year, in despair over his condition of leaking brain fluid, in despair over being dumped by his fiancée. But Anne had changed all that. The entire family loved Anne for bringing Justin back to us. And to top it all off, Anne was having a baby. That made her golden for our mother, Amelia. Another grandchild to love. Anne had brought another young lady into the Cameron fold, her sister Natalie. Natalie was a joy, a teenager who was completely lacking in that teenage angst, at least so far. Natalie was in remission from leukemia and would remain so, if the Cameron family had anything to say about it.

"Alex. Which ones do you think would be viable?"

I wanted to give him the old college standby, I agree with what's already been said, but I'd never get that chestnut past Hunter.

"Sorry. Wasn't really paying attention. Do you need a decision on these tonight or can I take them to the island with me, and Susan and I can go over them together?"

"I guess I could wait twenty four hours. I'll email everything to you. But get back to me by tomorrow night. It's been great but I have to get home."

"It wouldn't be six weeks since Liz had the baby, would it?" Justin asked with a sly grin.

Hunter's grin was genuine. "Six weeks today. See you later, bros." He turned around and was out the door.

Justin rose, but I grabbed his arm. "Why is it important that Liz had the baby six weeks ago?"

"Honestly, Alex, you need to get out in the world more. Six weeks is generally the time when it's considered safe for a woman to have sex after she's given birth."

"The things I'm learning."

"You better learn a few more things if you're going to keep your drop-dead gorgeous assistant dangling on your line."

"She's not dangling, I am."

"Well, get busy, bro. You have the Cameron reputation to uphold. If all else fails, get her pregnant. It worked for me."

"That implies marriage."

"Well, hell yeah, usually. Don't you want to marry her?"

"No."

"Oh," said Justin, holding up his hands, "I don't even want to go there. You brought her to Madeline's christening. Everyone thought you were showing us that you were going to make her a part of the family."

"I can't do that."

"My advice to you? If you can't marry her, let her go, bro. From the look of her at our family party, I'd say she's already in love with you. If you're not thinking marriage…you'd better not be thinking sex. She's the marrying kind."

"I can't marry her."

"It's your party," Justin said. "But I don't get it. Why don't you want to marry her? She's a perfect candidate to be part of the Cameron menagerie."

"There's nothing wrong with her. I…it's nothing. I should never have brought it up with you."

Winning Alex

I gathered up my coat and thought how to distract Justin from this unfortunate conversation. "Go home to your wife and hold her head."

"She only throws up in the morning."

"Well, go home to your wife and hold her hand. And while you're at it, tell her you love her." I shrugged into my coat and hurried out of the café. Outside in the cold, I clicked the button to unlock my car. Once inside, I gripped the steering wheel and then I rammed my head down on it. Hard.

Chapter 7

Susan

I did not finish those contracts by twelve o'clock. It was one fifteen in the morning by the time I was done. Then, just to make things interesting, as I walked home a chilly rain pelted me all the way. Yup, it rains in Rochester in the winter. Such a nice combination, rain, then snow. Maybe if I were really lucky, I'd catch pneumonia and get a couple of days off work.

When the morning came, I rose, knowing I had the trip to the Caribbean ahead of me. I told myself to eat something, but myself said, *not a good idea. Stomach a little queasy.* I put it down to the fact that I hadn't had much sleep and that I was going to be subjected to another whole day in Alex's company on a tropical island.

It was a silent ride on the plane and after we transferred to a smaller plane, a bit of a choppy landing. I gathered up my things, feeling a little nauseated. I've never been a good flier and the jouncing around we took gave me a huge case of nerves. I kept thinking I'd heard somewhere that small planes had the most crashes.

I gathered up my coat and my overnight bag and followed Alex out of the plane. At the bottom of the stairs, the heat hit my already queasy stomach like a blast from an oven. It had been eighteen degrees when we left Rochester. Now a sudden plunge into eighty-five degrees under brilliant sunshine was a large shock to my system. On top of it, I seemed to be disoriented. I grasped the rail, trying to fight my feeling of vertigo.

"You don't look well. Are you all right?" Alex asked.

I took a couple of steps forward and had the distinct feeling I was going to pass out. I gripped his arm, I couldn't help it, it was the only thing available. By sheer force of will I managed to stay upright. "The plane ride…I seem to be sick to my stomach."

My overnight bag was wrenched from my hand as well as my coat. Even burdened with my stuff and his, Alex gripped my elbow and escorted me up the four steps to the hotel where we always stayed. He checked us in and pushed me into the elevator. I remember him leading me into the bedroom, taking my shoes off and pushing me to lie down while he pulled a light cover over me to protect me from the air-conditioning. I remember him holding my head up and urging me to drink some nasty tasting stuff that he said would make me feel better which I promptly ran to the bathroom and regurgitated.

After the storm passed, Alex cleaned my face and hands with a cool wash cloth and told me three times how sorry he was. He carried me back to bed and said he was going to send for a doctor. I told him no. I didn't want some strange man poking and prodding me when I knew all I had was Betsy's flu. After that, I don't remember anything.

Alex

She's so sick. I felt so bad that I'd given her a pink concoction that the pharmacist said would make her feel better. It just made her sicker.

She's sleeping now. To top it all off, it's raining, a tropical rain that plops on the wide leaves of the banana trees outside the hotel. So I'm sitting next to her bed, watching her breathe, making sure she's still alive. I tell myself she'll be all right. In all the time she's worked for me, I've never known her to be unwell.

Sick as she is, she is still stunningly beautiful. Her skin is so clear, her lashes about a hundred miles long, dark and lying against her cheek. After she threw up the first time, I didn't try to undress her. I knew the best thing for her was to lie down on the bed and be absolutely still. I shot a text to Hunter, saying that Susan was ill and I doubted that we'd get the inspection done tomorrow on the hotel. I wasn't going to leave Susan alone until she was over this whatever it was. I assumed it was the flu. I dragged a big old leather lounge chair in from the living area and put it next to Susan's bed. Then we both slept.

Susan stirred and looked as if she were going to wake up. I looked at my watch. Eight o'clock in the evening. I needed to take my medication.

Inside my own suite, I swallowed the requisite four pills. A quick calculation told me that if we stayed beyond tomorrow, I would be out of medication. Not a good thing. We needed to go over that hotel tomorrow and get the hell out of here.

Susan

The inside of my mouth tasted vile. It took me a minute to remember where I was. Then the memories came back, very unwelcome memories of Alex holding my head while I vomited. What a romantic moment in the Caribbean. I felt like my fever was gone and the flu bug with it. It didn't last long, but it sure as heck was bad while it lasted. In the darkness, I could see the chair where Alex must have slept. I had just started to try an experimental stand up, when Alex appeared in the doorway.

He came to me at once and put a hand on my arm to steady me.

"How do you feel?"

"Better than I did a few hours ago. Alex, I'm so sorry…"

"Sorry for throwing up? Don't be ridiculous. Besides, you missed me. Did you want to try again?"

"Alex, I'm in a weakened state. I can't bear it when you're being charming and funny. It just reminds me how much I…like you."

"Susan. Dear, sweet Susan." He gathered me in his arms as if I were a child. I lay my head on his shoulder, trying to draw some strength from him.

He pulled away from me a little bit. "Do you think you could eat something?"

"Maybe. What I really need is a shower and a toothbrush."

"I think you'll find those accommodations in the bathroom. Then, if you like, I can order a light supper from room service and we can eat it here."

"That's an excellent idea."

Showered, hair washed and teeth brushed, I emerged from the bathroom wearing a hotel bathrobe and feeling almost human again.

It looked as if Alex had taken advantage of my absence and gone to his own suite to shower and shave. He looked wonderful in his white shirt and khaki pants, which I decided must be his island uniform.

The food arrived and Alex took charge of setting it up at the small dining table in front of the window that overlooked the street. He pulled out my chair so I could sit down and then he seated himself. I couldn't believe I could be with him like this, as if we were an old married couple sharing a meal in a way we'd done a hundred times before. The lack of sexual tension between us was quite unusual. Maybe I was still under the weather. Anyway, it was quite pleasant.

"You stayed with me all day," I said. "You could have gone to check out the project."

"I could have," he said easily, "but I didn't. I needed to make sure you were all right. Besides, it was an opportunity for me to catch up on my sleep. I guess you could say we were sleeping together."

He had that look that he got when he was more relaxed, that teasing, speculative look.

I said, "If you gave people the correct version, nobody would believe you."

"What do we care what people believe?"

"We don't, I guess." I realize when it came to Alex, I would do anything he wanted and not give a damn what people thought.

I'd filled my plate with pineapple and mango chunks and lovely squares of cheese. There were crackers too, in odd shapes of clovers and stars, and I thought it might behoove me to eat a couple to help my stomach settle. He'd ordered sparkling water instead of wine, and I drank thirstily from my glass.

"You know," I said, "I've noticed that about men. They are not nearly as sensitive to what people think as we women are. I think we're programmed from birth to seek approval."

"That doesn't sound like fun," he said in a casual tone.

"It isn't," I said, thinking of things that were said about me at my old job, that I'd encouraged Myer in order to be promoted and get a raise and I deserved what I got. I remembered how much those words hurt me.

"What do you think the answer is?" Alex asked, as if he were really interested in my opinion.

"I don't honestly know. It's a conundrum. We want women to be sensitive and caring, because they are raising the children, but on the other hand, it would be nice if they had a little bit more of a tough hide so life wouldn't bruise them so easily."

"Have you been bruised?"

I was sorry I started this conversation. I didn't want to remind him of my experience with Myer. Mostly I didn't want to think of Myer when I was here enjoying a lovely repast on a Caribbean island with a man I thought the world of.

"Bruises heal. Mine did." I plucked a banana from the fresh fruit dish and began to peel it. "What's the schedule for tomorrow?"

"Tomorrow we have breakfast, check out the project and head for home."

"So soon."

His eyes flickered downward and I had the distinct impression he was prevaricating. "Hunter wants this report as soon as possible."

It was on the tip of my tongue to say, "You could email it to him," but I didn't. Maybe Alex wanted to get away from this island before I threw myself at him.

When he'd finished eating, he slapped his thighs in that way he had, and rose. "I've got some things to wrap up. It's good to see you like your old self. Let's meet in the morning. About seven?"

"Sounds good," I said. But it didn't. I wanted him to spend the night with me, but that obviously was not in the cards.

When he was about to go out the door, I said, "Alex."

"Yes?"

"Thank you for taking such good care of me."

"You're my favorite assistant. Can't get along without you."

We both smiled, because being his favorite assistant was easy, since I was his only assistant. Then he stepped through the door and was gone.

I had trouble getting to sleep that night, I supposed because I'd slept for most of the day. Finally, about one o'clock I dozed off.

I came awake with a start and looked at the digital hotel clock. Three-thirty. Something was wrong…I felt it in my bones, like a mother knows when there's a problem with her child. I wrapped myself in a robe and went to the connecting door to Alex's room. I stood there listening. I couldn't hear anything. I almost went back to bed, but something made me open the door and step through.

Alex's bed looked as if we had had lively sex last night. Covers on the floor, sheet rumpled at the foot of the bed. Alex lay at angle on the bed, his chest bare, his briefs slung low over his hips. He wasn't moving at the moment, but by the look of the bed, he certainly had been scrabbling around. I went and laid my hand on his forehead. He was burning up. He'd caught my flu…or maybe something more virulent. Like a striking cat, he came up off the bed and grabbed my hand.

"Alex, it's Susan." He held me in a fierce grip. His eyes were glassy. I don't think he was really awake. "Alex, you're ill. Let me call a doctor."

"No."

"Then let me get some ice for your forehead."

"No. Just…stay."

I wrenched my hand loose and went into the next room to the ice bucket I knew would be sitting on the small table next to the little frig. I got a towel, put some ice in it, and went back to Alex.

"You never do what I tell you to." he mumbled.

"You know that's not true. I'm the most dutiful assistant you've ever had." I arranged the ice and the towel around his forehead. "I'll stay with you, if that's what you want me to do."

I went around to the other side of the bed and crawled in next to him. His body heat was intense. "Alex, please let me call a doctor."

In answer, he found my hand and gripped it so tightly that I almost doubted that he was sick. I pulled the sheet over me and found a spot that wasn't damp with his perspiration. I was doing what he wanted me to do, staying with him, not calling a doctor. But was it the right thing? I lay there looking up at the ceiling fan going round and round. Had I been the one to give him this sickness? It seemed the only logical conclusion. I went back in my memory to see where Alex had touched me. Yes. He'd held my head up to drink that awful stuff that I promptly threw up. He'd helped me clean up. Was that enough to make him this sick? This stuff must be really contagious.

It was perhaps an hour later when his breathing smoothed out. He was asleep. As I relaxed and my terrible tension left me, I felt sleep overtake me as well.

When I awoke, it was light, about eight o'clock. I discovered Alex, still asleep, had snuggled right next to me. His arm was thrown over my waist. His chest felt cool. His fever had broken, thank heaven. As much as I wanted to stay right here, close to him, I knew the best thing for him was to ease out from under his arm and let him get some much needed sleep. When I made a slight movement, his arm tightened. "Don't go," he said huskily.

"Alex, you've been ill…"

"Just let me lie here and feel what it would be like to wake up next to you."

His words seared my soul. I raised up enough to look down into his blue eyes. "It would be wonderful," I said, "it would always be wonderful." I had on a thin, low cut nightie and, as I leaned down to kiss him, I felt the hardness of his chest on my breasts. I took his mouth slowly, wanting to give him the chance to refuse my kiss if he didn't feel like accepting it.

He felt like it. His tongue came seeking mine and we played the game of hide and seek, he retreating into his mouth for me to chase him, me doing the same. I wanted him so much that shamelessly, I crawled on top of him. Like a scheming vixen, I knew he might not be so able to refuse me when he was in a weakened condition. Well, not that weak. He was hard and ready. I wriggled down enough on his body so I could take him in my mouth. I wrapped my hand around his root and suckled him, teasing him with my tongue, bringing his supple skin up and down.

I swirled my tongue around his tip, making him groan my name in the throes of exquisite pleasure. Discovering that he liked that made me continue it with more energy "Susan. You are..." He grabbed at my shoulders to bring me up so he wouldn't come in my mouth. I wouldn't have cared, but I understood that he was being considerate of me. I held him while he came. When he relaxed, I got a wet towel from the bathroom and cleaned him with it. I lay back on my side of the bed, feeling a little bit guilty. I had taken advantage of him when he was in a weakened condition. I was shameless. I couldn't help it. I'd never loved anyone like I loved Alex. He lay supine next to me, probably hating me. I moved to crawl out of bed. He grabbed my arm. "You're not going anywhere." In the next instant, he came up on top of me and straddled me. While I came instantly alive with anticipation, he stared down at me with those laser blue eyes. In the light of the day, I could see and feel his intensity. "Lift up your gown."

He was extracting his revenge, but it was a lovely revenge. I did as he said. Balancing himself on his knees, he leaned down and suckled me, his tongue going round and round my nipple. I went up in flames. It was exquisite, this torture. His hand was at my other breast and my hips involuntarily rose, seeking more satisfaction. He sat up then, and there was a dark gleam in his eye that was predatory. I suppose men had been looking at a woman spread underneath them like this for ages.

"Susan. You have to wear panties to bed?"

They really weren't panties as such. It was like a bikini bottom, just a narrow strip of fabric. "They came with the top."

"Perhaps…I can work around them." He pushed the flimsy material aside and cupped my mound, preparing me. Then he teased me by dipping a finger inside me, slowly sliding it down and taking it out.

"Alex, please. I need more." I couldn't believe I was pleading with him.

"Oh, no, my fine lady. You, who would seduce a sick man, will take your punishment and like it."

Oh, how I loved this, he acting the part of a marauder, me his willing servant. He found my nub and teased it. Sensation flooded my body, but it wasn't enough. Oh, it wasn't enough. He was torturing me deliberately with his slow hand in and out. He leaned over and took my breast in his mouth, even while he kept me teetering on the edge with his exploring fingers. Then his mouth left my breast. He leaned over me, his dark hair brushing my abdomen. Then I felt it, the warm, wet exquisite pleasure of his tongue on my nub. I cried out his name. He explored, he suckled, he lapped. His tongue took me over and over again, until at last I exploded in an orgasm of such power that I thought I was dying. He lifted his head and cupped my mound with his hand, sustaining my orgasm. He was the complete lover, edgy, daring, considerate. And I loved him completely.

He leaned down and kissed me, then rolled off me. "I think it's shower time."

I wondered if we were going to shower together, but he went inside his bathroom and closed the door. I took that as a no. I went back through my connecting door and climbed into my own shower. I knew I should regret what just happened. We'd danced around our attraction for each other for so long and now we'd given in. Not completely, but still. Was it going to be awkward…or better?

Evidently it was going to be exactly the same as it was. When I'd washed my hair and donned a light swing dress in a shade of blue I'd always liked, Alex strolled into my suite dressed in a light blue shirt and khaki pants, papers and laptop in hand. He laid his burden on the table and looked at me. "You look nice. Refreshed. Good shower?"

"Good shower," I said.

"Ready to work?"

"Of course," I said, feeling like Alice after she fell down the rabbit hole. This seemed to be another dimension.

We walked to the hotel. It was warm but there was an evocative island breeze. My body was alive, sensitive, feeling every movement of air across my skin. I was still feeling the effects of having a climax after so many years of deprivation. And yet, if I looked at Alex, it seemed as if it had all been a dream, it had never really happened.

We poked around all the corners of the new renovation. It seemed to be right on track and yet something was off. Because I spent a lot of my spare time looking at house accessories, faucets, door trims, light switch plates, I began to look more closely at these details.

"Alex." I motioned for him to come in to one of the bathrooms on the second floor. "These fixtures are supposed to be good quality chrome. Not…whatever these are. And the switch plates are wrong. Somebody is swapping out the original faucets and switch plates for cheap substitutes."

"You're right. Good eye. Let's take pictures, write it up and get out of here."

I've never made an exit from an island so fast. Alex ordered up the plane, told me to get packed. In forty five minutes we had taken off and were headed up into the blue skies.

Rochester was socked in under a heavy overcast and seemed exceptionally dark to me, after being on a sunny island.

At the airport, Alex told me to take a cab and go home, he wouldn't need me for the rest of the day. But I looked back to see that Lynne had come to meet Alex. She was supposed to be in New York City. What was she doing here? She looked upset as she handed him a small package. I couldn't imagine what that was all about.

"You are an idiot." Pretty as she was, my sister Lynne could be a bulldog when it came to her family.

I knew I'd be in for a tongue lashing from Lynne, but it couldn't be helped. I had to take that medication as soon as possible and she was the only one I could ask to bring it to me. None of the rest of the family were aware of my condition.

"Why didn't you take enough with you?"

"I didn't think we'd be gone more than twenty-four hours."

"Don't let this happen again. I will not lose you like we did Dad. And I wish you'd tell the rest of the family that you have the same condition Dad had. I'm getting tired of being the secret keeper."

"Just give me a little more time. Mom is so happy now with one grandchild and another on the way. I don't want to rain on her parade. Particularly since it will bring back her sorrow at losing Dad."

"You know you have to stay on a strict regime of medication."

"Yes, nurse, I'm well aware of my limitations."

"What about Susan? Have you told her?"

"Are you serious? God, no. Why on earth would I tell her?"

"You're going to marry her, aren't you?"

"And put her through what Mom went through when she lost Dad? No way. Not a chance."

"Alex, don't be such a prick. Susan loves you. It's written all over her face whenever she looks at you. How long do you think you can hold out against a woman who is perfect for you and adores you?"

"Not very long, it would seem."

"You haven't…"

"No, I haven't. Just some intense…petting."

"You need to be honest with her. Either tell her the truth, that you're a scared little rabbit and you're afraid to marry her because you might die on her, but you want to marry her anyway, or cut her loose."

"I can't lose her. She's a marvelous assistant. She's smart and quick and…"

"Beautiful," Lynne said, "don't forget beautiful."

The vision of Susan, that filmy nightgown up around her neck, her lovely breasts and lovely…everything exposed to me flashed through my mind. "She is that."

"I know you, Alex. And I think I know Susan. You're both young adults in the prime of your lives. Neither one of you is going to be content with "intense petting" for very long. Trust me, I know."

It was later, in the privacy of my condo, that I admitted to myself that Lynne was right. I would have to somehow put Susan out of my private life, but keep her in my professional one. How the hell am I going to do that?

I was distracted from my own dilemma by a family crisis. Toward the end of August, Justin's wife Anne went into the hospital to have her baby. She had planned to have a natural birth but there were complications and the doctors decided to do a Caesarean. We were all there in the waiting room, Hunter holding his baby daughter Madeline,

Liz, Mother Amelia, and Natalie, Anne's sister, when Justin came out to tell us of the doctor's decision. He was nearly beside himself. He was worried about Anne and worried about the baby. Liz was the first to come forward and enfold him in her arms and tell him everything would be all right, that it was a common procedure. Hunter, being the responsible patriarch asked him if Justin wanted a specialist flown in. Justin shook his head.

"There are already three doctors in there with her. I don't think she needs another one. They all know her from her time of working here and they are doing everything they can to make sure she and the baby will be okay. I just…" He shook his head. "If anything happens to her…"

I went to him and gave him a guy hug. "Listen to me, bro. What Anne needs from you now is to be strong. Go in there with a positive mind set. Nothing is going to happen to her or the baby. She's in good hands. But she needs you by her side. Go get those scrubs on and get in there with her. You can do this."

"You're only saying that because you've never done it."

I did a fake punch to his abdomen. "Don't be such a wuss. Man up."

He gave me a look like I'd pay for that insult later, but he took a breath and marched through the double doors.

The baby was born two hours later, a boy. Before very long, Justin beckoned us into the room where Anne was lying to show off his baby. The boy was blond, like Justin, with the hugest, bluest eyes I've ever seen on a newborn. This kid was going to be a lady killer. Justin picked up the sleeping baby and cradled him in his arms. "We're going to call him Josh."

"Congratulations, bro," I said. I had such conflicting feelings looking at Justin with his son in his arms. It was the largest responsibility there was. And God help me, I wanted it.

Justin beckoned to Natalie, Anne's sister who'd been looking wistfully on from a distance. Justin and Anne had formally adopted the teenager a few weeks ago. "Would you like to hold your little brother?"

Natalie's eyes lit up. "Can I?"

In answer, Justin put the baby into Natalie's arms. I was glad I was there to see that young girl's joy, but now I felt that we all needed to go and leave the young family alone. My mother Amelia lingered.

"What do you think, Ma?" Justin asked cheekily.

Winning Alex

Amelia didn't even bother to give him the usual reprimand. She just reached up and kissed him on the cheek. "I love you," she said. 'Thank you for my grandson." Justin murmured back. "You are welcome. And I love you too, Ma. You can hold the baby after Natalie."

My mother smiled. "I can wait."

Chapter 8

In the three days before Thanksgiving, in the office, Alex was just as he always was, cool, formal. I'd heard that he had a new nephew, Justin and Anne's son, Josh. I congratulated him on the addition to his family.

When I tried to broach the subject of what had happened on the island between us, I did it obliquely, asking him if Hunter was able to correct the filching that was going on at the renovated hotel. He gave me that cool, expressionless Alex look and said, "I haven't discussed it with him, but I presume so." And that was the end of that. Except that he announced that I was to have the entire weekend off.

An entire weekend off? I hadn't had an entire weekend off since I started working for him. That meant I would go for three whole days without seeing him. I had that horrible feeling that he was freezing me out.

On the weekend, I tried to be a good daughter and eat Mom's food. She's a wonderful cook, but I couldn't eat very much. I was one big bundle of nerves. Mom is a gem. She didn't ask me anything, just looked at me with those worried Mom eyes and said, "Whatever it is that is bothering you, you know you can always talk to me."

"Thanks, Mom," I said.

But I knew I wasn't going to share my dilemma with her. I couldn't. She'd be too worried.

On Saturday, as an antidote to my agonizing over what I should or shouldn't have done, should or shouldn't have said, I asked Betsy to come over. About eight o'clock, she blew into my apartment like a refreshing winter breeze, bringing sanity with her.

We had agreed on pizza. She liked black olives, so I ordered a half black olives, all pepperoni and cheese. What did I care if I gained weight?

"Well," I said, when the pizza was delivered and we were devouring it. "Are you leaving for the opal mine in Australia?"

"I don't know. Sam doesn't know what to do. He's really tempted by the money. I hate to think I might end up living in a hole in the ground in some god-forsaken place."

I looked around the apartment. It seemed as if I'd been holed up here for far too long. "You know what? We need to go out. Have a drink. Go where the bright lights are."

"Excellent idea." She looked down at her jeans. "I'm not very dressed up."

We both had on the uniform of casual, jeans and a t-shirt. "Don't worry about it. Nobody dresses up these days."

We entered Chez Louie's to find it already packed with revelers. We found one empty stool at the bar. I pushed Betsy to sit down and I'd stand behind her. At the back of the bar, instead of a mirror, the owner had mounted the hood of a red Chevrolet pick-up truck circa 1947. When Betsy and I ordered a beer, the bartender drew our drinks from spigots mounted under the chrome grill. I scanned the room. There was a guy with a minicam on his shoulder following another man with a microphone in his hand. It looked like they were doing spontaneous interviews. Being in the business of selling and buying and promotion, I guessed this must be a gimmick by the owner to garner free advertising.

I paid for the drinks while Betsy swung around to clink her glass mug to mine. "Here's to us," she said. "BFFs forever."

We both drank. I tried to relax and pretend this was my thing, but truth to tell I hadn't gone pub crawling since I started to work for Alex. Betsy sat up and gave her full attention to something over my shoulder. "Say, isn't that your boss?"

I looked. It was Alex, all right, as I had never seen him. He wore a tux under his Burberry coat, the white tie tied precisely, above a snowy white shirt front. Clinging to his arm was a woman who could only have been a super model. Perhaps not now, since she was older, but she must have been once, with those high cheek bones and that stylish hair cut curling over her left eye. And those long, long legs. The camera must have loved them. She was almost, but not quite, as tall as Alex. She wore a white faux fur coat and a clingy black dress underneath it. They looked a little out of place here where everyone else was dressed casually. The bistro went a little quieter as people checked them out. I was having trouble breathing.

Microphone man spied Alex. He was, after all, hard to miss.

"Mr. Cameron. How nice to see you. And your lovely companion. Would you introduce us?"

I knew Alex would rather eat nails than be caught in this kind of spot light. But when I expected him to push the rude guy aside, Alex glared into the bright light of the camera and said, "This is Collette." The woman nodded politely to the interviewer.

"Are you a friend of Mr. Cameron's..." he hesitated and then said slyly, "or are you something more?"

"Mr. Cameron and I have known each other for...a while. More I cannot say."

"How about it, Mr. Cameron? Will we hear wedding bells ringing soon?"

"If you do," Alex growled, "you should get your ears checked."

Alex took hold of the incredibly slender woman and guided her straight toward me. I think he was \a little blinded from the camera's bright light.

Out of the deep well of anger and hurt, I pulled courage. If he thought he was going to walk by without acknowledging me, he had another think coming.

"Hello, Mr. Cameron."

He stared at me as if he didn't know me.

I said in my sweetest most sycophantic voice, "I hope you had a nice Thanksgiving with your family."

He still stared at me, but finally he got himself together enough to say, "Very nice, thank you. Now if you'll excuse us..."

When they had walked by me, I heard "Collette" say, "Alex, who was that girl?

Not woman. Girl. I couldn't hear what Alex answered. He put his hand on "Collette's" back and guided her to a private booth out of sight of the hoi polloi.

"So." Collette's husband Giovanni rose from the booth. "How was the ballet?"

"Wonderful." She turned to Alex. "Thank you for taking me. It's so nice to have an escort who is not fidgeting in his seat like my husband does, dying for it to be over."

"My pleasure," Alex said, thinking he wished very much that they had not been spotted by the media...and Susan. What must she think?

I stood very still. I did everything I could to stave off the pain. I wanted numbness. But finally the pain broke through, like water rushing through a hole in the dam. And it hurt very, very badly. I could not believe he would date a has-been super model after all we'd shared.

"Hey, hey," Betsy said. "You can't think he really cared for that woman? She was eye candy...well maybe she was eye candy past the sell-by date. But he must see women like her frequently."

"He's never dated a woman like that. Not in the time I've worked for him." What a fool I'd been to think he could care for me. We'd shared a little play time together…and that's all it was. Playtime.

I felt really stupid. I put my beer glass on the counter very carefully and said to Betsy, "Do you mind if we go?"

"Good idea." She drained the last of her drink and slid off the stool.

I had used my car to go to the club. I delivered her back to my loft so she could pick up hers.

Betsy said, "I don't know what to say. I can tell you're really hurt. I'm so sorry."

"Don't be," I said. "I've just had a major dose of one of life's important lessons. Now if I could just figure out what it was."

Betsy gave me a hug, stepped out into the cold and hurried to her car. I watched to see that she got the motor started, then I headed to my loft.

So it had happened. I'd given my body…and my heart to a man who…who what? I couldn't even think of a word for it. It wasn't betrayal. There had been no promises asked, none given. And yet he'd stayed with me when I was sick and I had done the same for him. I still remembered the heat in that bed, the lazy turn of the fan overhead, the exquisite pleasure of bringing him to climax and when he returned the favor, crying out with overwhelming sensual release under his hand.

I went through the ritual of getting ready for bed, showering, brushing my teeth, doing everything I could to get the scent of liquor and perfume off my skin, trying to scrub away the memory. I climbed into a pair of flannel pajamas and went to bed to stare up at the ceiling. Having a loft downtown meant if you didn't have curtains over the windows, there was always light streaming in from the street lamps. So the light played over my beloved industrial heat runs. And I finally let myself think about my dilemma. What was I going to do?

I had three choices. I could go to work and act as if nothing had happened. I could go to work and give my two weeks' notice. Or I could go to work and confront Alex. Number one would be the safe thing to do. Number two would be disastrous, both to my psyche and to my bank account. Number three was extremely dangerous.

I decided I wasn't in a good frame of mind to make a decision. I only knew that if I quit, which seemed the most viable option emotionally, I would lose my wonderful loft and my equally wonderful salary. Worst of all, I would lose all contact with Alex. I needed to step back and give myself some time to recover.

In the end, I decided to go with option number one for now. It wouldn't hurt to go to work and simply act as if nothing had happened, at least for a week or two. I was sure Alex would never bring up anything about his sudden desire to date an out of date model.

I was right. Alex simply announced that there would be an acquisition meeting at ten o'clock and Hunter wanted me there. I'd been included in these meetings before, but my focus had always been on Alex. Now I wanted my attention to be anywhere but on him, so I studied his two brothers. Hunter seemed older, more mature than he had a year ago. Having a wife and family had had a calming influence on him, I thought. Justin sprawled back in his leather chair. He still looked like a mischievous teenager, although he was just a few years younger than Alex. His blond good looks were such a contrast to his brothers. Then my eyes went to Alex. I couldn't help it. His face was a face that drew the eye, so well-proportioned as it was. I tried not to think about how he had looked leaning over me, touching me. But the more I tried not to think, the more I remembered how he'd suckled my breasts and brought me to climax.

"Susan? Do you have any thoughts to share with us?" Hunter asked.

Share my thoughts with you? Not in this lifetime. I sat up and tried to look intelligent. "I'm just wondering how much money you want to sink into the two chanciest projects, the one in Iowa and the one in Pennsylvania. They seem off the beaten path to me. Will there be a buyer for them?"

"I believe I just mentioned that I had a buyer for both of them," Hunter drawled, his eyes dancing.

Oh, boy. Totally caught out. I tried to recover. "Well, then, that's all right."

"Any thoughts on the other properties?" Hunter's mouth quirked. He was enjoying himself.

I said, "No, no thoughts."

When the meeting was over, I fled the room. I'd decided I was going to eat lunch out. Let the man who dates models get his own damn sandwich.

I had thrust one arm through the sleeve of my coat when Alex came out of his office. "You're going out to lunch?" he said.

"Yes," I said.

"Are you meeting someone?"

I just stared at him. I couldn't believe he was asking me that question. He said, "I just thought if you weren't meeting anyone, we could go out together."

"Yes. I am meeting someone." Which of course was a lie.

"Oh. Well, have a good lunch then."

The idiotic man stood watching me as I gathered up my purse and walked down the hall. Kenneth Johnson was coming out of his cubicle just as I passed. I grabbed his arm and said under my breath, "Walk with me to the elevator, will you?" I smiled up at him as I said it. He was confused but game. "Sure," he said. "I'm going that way anyway."

Alex

Justin wandered into my office and sat on the corner of my desk. If there was anything I didn't want, it was a cozy chat with the brother who was the most perceptive of the three of us.

"Not going out for lunch?" He picked up a paperweight from my desk and appeared to be absolutely engrossed with the fleur de lis pattern embedded in the bottom.

"No." I thought if I was rude, he would leave. I should have known better. He knew me too well. My obvious unwillingness to talk to him just egged him on.

"You know, none of us can figure out what's wrong with you. You've been like a bear with a sore head since you came back from that last Caribbean trip. We all know you've fallen hard for your hot babe assistant, but we can't figure out why that should make you so grouchy. Mother's worried about you, and frankly so am I."

"Don't you mean Ma?" I asked with a touch of irony in my voice.

"I only call her that to her face. She loves it."

She probably did. Unlike most mothers, she reveled in all her children's quirky traits. She had always enjoyed Justin's pranks and his ability to poke holes in pompous people. I suspected Justin got his sharp tongue from her side of the family, since his blond good looks came from his mother's male line of nobility.

"I remember the time when we were close, Alex. We used to pull some good jokes on Hunter. Now you're just…all business. And frankly bro," he put the paper weight down and slid off the desk. "I liked you better when you were helping me gang up on big brother. Sooner or later, you're going to have to tell us what's eating you. Mother's not going to stand for too much more of your sour face."

"I don't have a sour face."

"Look in the mirror. You'd be surprised at what you see. I'm going to get something to eat. I suggest you do the same. Might improve your temper."

Nothing was going to improve my temper. Particularly after seeing Susan walk out with Kenneth Johnson. That man was entirely too friendly with all the female employees who worked in this office. On a couple of occasions, I'd been on the point of calling him up on the carpet to talk to him. Hunter counseled me against it. If he wasn't really stepping out of line, if he was just talking to a woman on his break time, I had no right to interfere.

Office politics. Always tricky.

I suppose that my appearing with Collette in that pub had shocked Susan. I thought about explaining that she was a friend with whom I attended the ballet once a year, and we were meeting her husband, but that sounded lame even to me. I hated the cool, controlled look on her face when she came into the office this morning to go over my schedule with me. Maybe it was a blessing in disguise. I'd wanted distance, hadn't I? Well, I got it in spades.

Chapter 9

Susan

I got through the week somehow. When the weekend came, I decided there would be no more pub crawling for me. If Alex was going to date his gorgeous women, he'd have to do it without me watching.

Besides, I had other excitement. Sam had taken the job in Cobber Pedy and Betsy was getting married next weekend, not in the spring as she had planned. She'd decided that she was going to go with Christmas colors and she wanted me to wear red. I was more than happy to oblige. With my brown hair and brown eyes, I needed to wear a strong color.

At work, I was often on the phone with her, helping her plan the wedding and reception. Alex would come out of his office with a contract to go over or an estimate of reno work he wanted me to check and he would have to stand and wait until I cut off my conversation. The bachelor party was my responsibility. I thought I'd have it in my loft. There was plenty of room for all her female friends. Yeah, unlike me, she had female friends. There would be twenty-five of them all together. I didn't have time to cook and wasn't skilled in that department anyway, so I made all the arrangements while I was at work. I called a caterer and luckily, found one who had had a cancellation and was available on such short notice. I also hired a couple of male strippers. I'd just finished with that call when Alex came out of his office looking pretty much like a thundercloud.

"Miss Zalinsky."

"Yes, Mr. Cameron?" I couldn't believe how sweetly innocent I sounded.

"You seem to be making an extraordinary amount of personal calls."

"Yes, Mr. Cameron," I said. "And since it seems to be annoying you, I'm going to go home. I have quite a bit of vacation coming and I'm going to take it now. I won't be in the office for the next couple of days. That way I can make my calls from home and not disturb you."

"May I ask why you suddenly need personal time?"

"Of course you may ask," I said cheerfully. "I have a wedding to plan."

I walked out of the office feeling more lighthearted than I had felt in weeks.

Alex

She had a wedding to plan? She had a wedding to plan? What the hell did that mean? She couldn't be getting married. She didn't date anyone, at least not that I knew of. One lunch with Kenneth Johnson didn't lead to a wedding that fast. Or did it?

Susan

On the night of Betsy's bachelor party, my loft had never been so full of lively, three sheets to the wind women. The caterer had come with the food and laid it out on my island. It was a feast of finger foods, meat balls in sauce to spear on a toothpick, chips and dips, cold meats and cheeses, delicious freshly baked bread and strawberries to dip in a chocolate fountain. And of course lots and lots of wine. I tried to be a responsible host, but the women I'd been introduced to as Mary Dennis and Sweets Peterson declared the Pink Moscato wine I'd chosen to be divine and had availed themselves of it way too often. But they had a designated driver, so I wasn't really worried about them. I'd planned a game, but every time I tried to get the group quiet long enough to announce charades, they'd overruled me and said they wanted to see the stripper men. Where were the men?

I made a general announcement that the men would not be here until ten o'clock, that Betsy was going to open her presents first. While she was still on her feet, I thought. Betsy's favorite wine was Riesling and I'd lost count of how many glasses she'd had. Everybody groaned, but good naturedly gathered around the bride. Betsy sat in the lovely little chair that was the exact copy of the one Alex had in his office that I'd indulged in not long after that second raise. She looked like a princess with her blond hair long and curly, her blue eyes and her flushed cheeks. She had on a Christmas green dress in a silky fabric that crisscrossed her breasts and displayed how well- endowed she was. She began to open presents. I was designated to write everything down so she could send out thank you cards before she left for Australia.

Most of the gifts were filmy lingerie or teddies. I had told everyone I thought those were the best gifts. Betsy wouldn't be able to take kitchen appliances or anything like that with her. Unlike those of us who needed flannel in the middle of winter, those bits of nothing would be just the thing for the one hundred degree plus temperatures she was going to experience in the Australian desert. I had gifted her with a blue baby doll pajama set. She lunged toward me to hug me, scattering gift paper wrapping around her high heels. When all the gifts were open and all the thank yous said, I put on some dance music. Almost everyone was out on my hardwood floor, dancing to those old standards of R.E.S.P.E.C.T. and YMCA, songs that everyone knew the dance moves to. At a lull in the music, my doorbell rang out the big Ben chimes.

"It's the strippers," somebody cried, and they all went screaming to the door. I was rinsing out wine glasses and had my back to the room. When I turned around, I nearly lost it. They had dragged the man into the room and were busily tugging off his coat, ruffling his hair and pulling at his belt. The man they were stripping was Alex. I plunged into the gaggle of women around him and put my hands up. In my most authoritative voice I said, "Back off, ladies. This isn't one of the strippers. This is my boss."

There was silence for a moment. Then a voice piped up. "He could join them. He's beautiful enough."

Alex bowed his head. "A most intriguing proposition which unfortunately I must decline."

Another voice said, "Ooh, and he talks good, too."

"Again I thank you. However I feel that stripping is not in the area of my expertise. I came to talk to Susan."

"Lucky girl," someone muttered.

Just then, the two men who were the real strippers stepped into the room. "Is there a party here that needs a couple of sexy men?"

There were squeals and screams as the women rushed to their new targets. I told Mary...I hoped she could still read the labels on the music CDs...which one to put in the player.

The music started and the men boogied into the middle of the room. The taller one, Motorcycle Mike, said, "Let the party begin."

I grabbed Alex's arm and steered him toward my bedroom. I'd fantasized a million times about having him here, but not with a gaggle of screaming women and two male strippers on the other side of the wall.

"I've come at a bad time."

I laughed, I couldn't help it. His hair was mussed and his buckle was half undone. "You think?" The walls pulsed with the beat of the music. The screams were a little more muffled.

"This isn't...your bachelor party."

"No, it's my friend Betsy's. I apologize for my guests swarming over you like that. They're not entirely sober."

"I guessed as much. It wasn't...all that unpleasant. I've never been mistaken for a male stripper before. It was quite...exhilarating."

"I'm glad you weren't offended."

"Why should I be offended?"

"You are rather formal and stiff-necked."

"Is that how you see me?" He moved closer to me. I became aware that there was a huge bed in this room, even though it was covered with my guest's coats. The lighting was subdued, I'd only left on the two small lamps on my bed tables, thinking I needed the light if someone had to use the extra bathroom.

"Why are you here?" I asked.

"I'm not...quite sure."

"When will you know?"

"Maybe after I do this." He came to me and gathered me into his arms. He gave this funny little sigh, as if he'd been starved for the feel of me. I knew I was ravenous.

"Alex, are you going to kiss me, or are you going to stand there and think about it?"

"Choice number one," he said and he took my mouth eagerly, absorbing my tongue into his mouth, playing our game of hide and seek. He broke off the kiss and pressed my head into his shoulder. "Holy hell. I tried to stay away from you, I really did. But I kept thinking that if you were getting married…"

"Getting married? And just who would I be marrying?"

"Any man in his right mind." And he kissed me again, quite fervently. When he lifted his head he said, "How long is this bacchanalia going to last?"

"Probably till three or four in the morning."

He groaned. "I wanted to come back after it was over."

"Alex, you can't. I have to get a few hours sleep. Betsy is being married at noon tomorrow. Would you like to come to the reception?" I thought he'd have at least three objections.

"Yes," he said.

I told him where the reception was being held. "The doors are open at twelve thirty, but the bridal party won't be there until about one o'clock. We have to pose for pictures. I'm the maid of honor."

"Yes, you are," he breathed. "All right. I'll see you at Betsy's reception. I don't suppose there's a back way out of here."

Smiling, I shook my head. "Not unless you want to use the fire escape."

He raised an eyebrow. "First I get mistaken for a stripper, now you want me to turn me into a cat burglar?"

"Come on," I said. "I'll help you run the gauntlet and retrieve your coat."

"You are a lady and a scholar." He grabbed my hand and dragged me behind him. I protested. "Hey, I thought I was running interference."

"I'm bigger and taller," he said.

He didn't have to worry. The strippers were down to their tiny briefs by now and dancing for dollars. They had everyone's attention. I picked Alex's coat up off the floor and held it for him to shrug into. He gave me a quick, unsatisfying kiss. "I'll see you tomorrow."

"I'll see you tomorrow," I said, thinking how quickly my world had turned from dark to wonderful

Chapter 10

Betsy made an absolutely beautiful bride. She'd chosen a strapless, full skirted dress that made her look like a doll on a wedding cake. Sam, with his red hair and his stalwart features was a perfect masculine compliment to her blond femininity. When the wedding was over and the pictures had been taken, we were riding together to the reception in the wedding limo when Betsy whispered to me, "Did I dream it or did you say Alex is coming to the reception?"

She and Sam were in the back seat. Mike, Sam's best man and I rode facing them. "You didn't dream it," I said, smiling. "I hope you don't mind."

"Of course I don't mind. But shouldn't you mind? Did you ask him about his I'm-so-beautiful model?"

"No. and I probably won't."

Sam captured Betsy's chin and turned her face toward him for a long kiss. "We're married, babe. Can you believe it?"

"Not really. Love me?"

"Always," Sam said and kissed her again.

"You two need to get a room," Mike said, which made Betsy laugh.

Winning Alex

"Oh, my gosh. When we do get a room, it'll be legal."

"Imagine that," I said.

Betsy and Sam's guests were seated at the round tables scattered around the room. There was much clapping and cheering when the bride and groom appeared. I searched the room for Alex but he wasn't there. I tried to hide my disappointment as we were escorted to the bridal table. All through the reception I kept looking for him. He never came.

When it was time for Betsy and Sam to leave on their honeymoon to Niagara Falls, I kissed Betsy. "He didn't come, did he?" she whispered in my ear.

"No," I said, "he didn't come."

I drove home fighting back tears. It was like a double whammy. I would miss Betsy like crazy and Alex hadn't kept his promise.

I pulled in front of my loft and swung around to park my car on the correct street for Saturday night. I hadn't noticed the car parked ahead of me before, but now my headlights picked up color and make. It was a red Jeep.

I wrapped my coat around myself tightly, climbed out of the car and headed for my building. I was halfway across the street when he grabbed my arm and pulled me around to him. "Susan."

I looked up at him and said in the coolest tone I could, "Alex."

Snow fell on his dark head, glittering in the light of the street lamps.

"Do you think we could possibly get out of the middle of the street before we get run over?"

"You're the one who accosted me." I wrested my arm loose from his hold. "Where were you?"

"I…there was something I had to do."

"You always have something to do. Well, you can do it without me."

Seeing Betsy with Sam and then feeling the sharp disappointment of having Alex bail on me was too much. I didn't want to feel like this anymore. I didn't want to go on loving someone who had all the clarity of a Chinese puzzle. It was too damn tiring. "Go away," I said.

He followed me into the building and punched the elevator button. I said, "You might as well not come up. I don't want to see you anymore." In the elevator, I tried to pull the door shut before he got in but he was too quick for me.

"I thought you loved me," he said in that amused way he had.

"I'm tired of loving you," I said. "I can't love you anymore because I don't understand you. It's too wearing. I'm giving you my two weeks' notice now."

I tried to keep him from coming into my apartment, but I wasn't any more successful with that than I had been the elevator door.

He followed me in, closed the door and locked it. He took my coat and hung it up on the wall, and then he hung his coat up on the wall along with his white silk scarf.

By now, my heart was going wham, wham, but I told it to calm down. He was probably here to tell me he'd thought it over and we needed to go back to being business associates and nothing more. I could tell him he needn't bother. I would give up the loft and I'd go back to dispensing coffee before I'd subject myself to the torture of seeing him every day without his ever acknowledging the truth of how he felt about me.

I went into my kitchen and looked for something to bang around, a pot a pan, anything, but I was too neat. I had gotten up early and cleared away all the party debris in nervous anticipation of seeing Alex at the reception.

He came up behind me. His hands circled my waist and he pulled me into him, my back to his chest. "Have you got any spaghetti?"

"What?" I was going to kill him, I really was. My heart was breaking in a million pieces and he was talking about food. I turned around and tried to push him away. He wouldn't allow it.

"I had this fantasy about you and spaghetti."

"What, me cooking and you eating, the way any good little woman should take care of her man?"

"No," he said, and he lightly pushed my hair back from my face, "you and me naked…with maybe a little spaghetti in there somewhere."

It took me a minute, but I catch on quick. "This is crunch time, Mr. Cameron. If you don't have a condom in your pocket…"

"I come fully prepared." He kissed the side of my neck. "Did I tell you how much I like you in that red dress?" He kissed the v in my throat. "Did I tell you how much I'd like you if you weren't in that red dress?"

I pulled him close, feeling his erection, loving his erection. "Do you think we can make it to the bedroom?"

"We might just…" He step walked me to my bedroom door and when he reached the bed, he collapsed on it with me underneath him.

"Alex…about that woman you were with…"

"Her husband is a good friend of mine. I take her to the ballet every year. Her husband was in the booth waiting for us."

"You could have told me."

"I just did. Can we make this work…working together and being lovers?"

"I think we already have…well at least we did until I quit a few minutes ago."

"You did, didn't you?"

My dress had the same crisscross style as the dress Betsy had worn to her bachelor party. He pushed aside one strip of fabric to kiss me just at the top of my breast. "It's going to be hard for me to find a new assistant who can make the discovery of stolen switch plates and faucets as exciting as you do. And your contributions in the acquisition meetings. So insightful."

"All right. So I wasn't paying attention. I was fantasizing about you, you brat."

"I, a brat? I have it on good authority that I am beautiful enough to join a line of strippers and I talk good, too."

I laughed. "You talk real good, mister." I mimicked his bad usage.

He leaned over and kissed my throat right in the area of my voice box. His warm lips explored, going ever closer to my breast. "You kiss real good, too," I said, hardly able to breathe. I felt like I was in a dream. I had wanted this, ached for it so long, that now it was really happening and Alex was in my arms in my bed, I was almost afraid. I was afraid that when he entered me, my world would be forever changed. It was like stepping out on a high precipice. I might soar up to heaven…or I might fall down so far I could never get up again.

It started to rain. The sound of it pelting on my roof made me feel closed in with Alex.

He lifted up and looked down at me. "What is it?"

"It's raining."

"I like rain," he said. "Lying here with you I feel tucked in and cozy." He pushed aside the other strap of my dress and now I was completely bare to him. His eyes darkened. "You are…exquisite." He leaned over and took the tip of my breast in his mouth and my hips lifted involuntarily. My mind told me that if I was afraid that once I had sex with Alex, he would set me aside, I should stop this now, while I still could. My body had other ideas. He found the zipper on the side of my dress and slid it down, allowing me to shift my dress downward and off my legs. I lay in front of him wearing only my tiny thong and my thigh high stockings. He started on my left leg, rolling the stocking down slowly, deliberately, watching me every moment. The other leg received the same treatment. His hands were so warm, so masculine, so skilled. My thong had a snap on one side. He found it and with a sound of satisfaction, pulled it loose and stripped me of my last bit of underwear.

    He was still fully clothed. He put his hand over my mound and then his fingers found my nub. He teased and rubbed and explored, going a little further inside me each time. Then he suckled me, and I grabbed his shirt, feeling his muscled shoulders and wordlessly, pleaded with him to stop, pushing at him. I didn't want to come this way. I wanted him inside me, where he had never been. He ignored my tugging and went on pleasuring me, until I could no longer resist. Great waves of pleasure rolled over me and I arched my back and cried out my pleasure and came again and again. He cupped his hand on me to keep the wonderful torture racketing through my body.

When the storm had passed and I reached a form of sanity, I realized he was standing beside the bed fully clothed.

"Susan. Come here."

"I already have," I said smiling.

"Come again?" he asked in a sweet double entendre.

I rose up to my feet and stood in front of him completely nude. He made no move toward me. Instead, he let his gaze rove over me, taking in the swell of my breasts, my abdomen, the nest between my legs and my bare feet.

"I like you like this...like you're a painting by Goya. Are you feeling self-conscious?" he asked me.

It seemed an odd thing to ask me. "No," I said. "I don't think I could ever be self-conscious with you."

"Undress me." When I stood there wondering which delicious part of him I would start on first, he said, "That's an order...from your boss." His eyes sparkled with humor. I couldn't believe he was joking about the barrier that had kept us apart for so long. He held out his arm for me to undo his cuff links. While I worked at flipping the little catch, he touched my breast so tenderly, as if my nipple were the finest work of art. My fingers fumbled at that bit of gold in his sleeve. "Are you having trouble concentrating?" he asked in that smooth, self-assured voice.

"I'm having trouble breathing," I said, in a burst of honesty.

"So truthful. And here's your reward." He leaned over and kissed me, then took me in his mouth.

At last the cuff link came free and because Alex held me in place, loving my breast as it had never been loved before, I tossed the jewelry on my dresser. It hit the mirror with a little plink, but the mirror didn't break.

"Alex, I…need your other arm."

He raised his head, his face dark with sexual hunger. I almost had another orgasm just looking at him. He bent as if to favor my other breast with the same attention he'd given the first but I blocked him with my arm, much as I hated to. "No," I said. "I can get this done faster if you don't…"

More skilled now with the second cuff link, I slipped it out of the buttonhole and tossed it to join the first one. It too, hit the mirror.

"You break the mirror, you'll have seven years of bad luck."

"That's an old wives' tale."

"I've often wondered who these old wives are, haven't you?"

"Alex, I really don't care." Before he could touch me, I grabbed the shoulders of his shirt to tug it off and then realized I could effectively pin his arms to his sides. Holding him prisoner, I found his nipple and licked first one and then the other.

"Enjoying yourself?" he asked in the deep voice that held a touch of edginess in it, not making any move to free his arms.

"Immensely," I said. "You?" Still holding him captive, I licked my way down his chest to his navel and twirled my tongue in the cavity. He tasted salty.

"I'm quite…engaged in the proceedings."

Honestly. Did this man have to be erudite even while he was being sexually assaulted? I wondered if there was any way I could hold the shirt in place and unzip his pants to free him. I found I could, especially since he made no move to free himself. His member sprang free, hard and full. My insides clutched at the sight of it.

"Yes," I said. "I can see how "engaged" you are."

"Fully, you might say." He stood waiting, his arms still captured.

I bent to him. This man deserved to be tortured, and I was determined to do my best. I sent my tongue over the top of his member, just barely touching him. His groan was music to my ears. I licked a tad bit harder, circling the tip, lapping underneath it.

"Remind me to fire you in the morning," he groaned.

"You can't. I already quit."

"Don't…quit."

I knew he wasn't talking about work. I sucked the tip lightly, just barely taking it in my mouth. He didn't move, although I could feel the tension in his body as he fought not to push himself deeply in my mouth. I rewarded his restraint by taking him in more fully. I loved the taste of him, salty, male. I reveled in loving him with my tongue and my lips. I used my other hand to extend my capture of him. I had the entire length of him in my hand and my mouth. I could feel him struggling to hold back, but that only made me increase my sucking out his full length and then relaxing back. I found a rhythm, and before I could really take as much of him as I wanted, he grabbed my head and tried to pull me up. I resisted. He could no longer hold the storm back. He came in my mouth and I swallowed his cum.

He shrugged out of his shirt, undid his belt and shimmied out of his pants. He sat down on the bed and dispensed with his shoes and socks and was lying flat on his back in bed and pulling me down on top of him almost before I realized what was happening. "Damn." He rolled me off him to one side.

"What is it?"

"Condom's in my pants pocket."

"We won't need it right away, will we?"

"Don't bet on it," he said.

He lay down beside me, the packet in his hand. I took his other hand and brought it to my mouth. "You have beautiful hands," I said, and I sucked his index finger.

"What the hell are you doing?"

"Loving you," I said. "Haven't you ever had anyone love you like this, no holds barred, every part of your body accessible?"

"No," he said in a low husky voice. "No woman has ever been interested in my hands before."

"Ah," I said. "Then this is a new experience for you." I sucked his middle finger, gave it lots of nice laps.

"Susan. You..."

I crawled on top of him and held both his hands together over his head. "I used to imagine you were a pirate."

"Some pirate to allow himself to be captured like this. Not once, but twice."

I leaned forward and rubbed my breasts against his chest. "Are you ready to do my bidding?"

"Oh, yeah."

I let go of his hands and plucked the packet off his chest. He had to help me but together we got him sheathed. I'd put on a big act with all my play capturing of him, but now I was trembling. After an eternity of waiting, I was finally going to have Alex inside me. Where he belonged. Where he had always belonged.

It seemed odd that for our first time, Alex was going to let me remain on top of him and control how fast or slow I took him in. I tried for slow, I really did. But when I felt him inside me, so big, giving me that longed for fullness I'd wanted for an eternity, I couldn't hold back. I took him in to the hilt. And I did it again. And again. I arched above him and he clasped my breasts. I took him more and faster. The explosion came all at once, and I shattered. The ecstasy was more intense, more all-consuming than I had ever imagined it could be. Alex, too, was in the throes of his orgasm and his face was beautiful in his absorption with his complete pleasure. It increased my pleasure a thousand fold to know I had done that for him. Suddenly he rolled, putting me underneath him. He was lengthening his orgasm by taking control of our rhythm. I clutched his shoulders, wanting this moment to go on forever. We reached our peak together. In the aftermath of the storm, Alex lay on top of me. I realized this might be the awkward part. He leaned over and kissed me on the nose. Then he rose and went into the bathroom to dispose of his condom. I lay there, not wanting to pull the sheet up, not wanting anything to touch my body but Alex

Chapter 11

Alex came out and lay down beside me, propping his head up on his elbow so he could see me. "I don't want you to quit, Susan."

I didn't know whether to be hurt or happy. Why did his first thought have to be about our business relationship?

"So you want me to come to work and pretend this never happened?"

"Of course not. I'm not an idiot. I'm just saying that I want you to continue to be my assistant. "

"And what about this?" I was upset, I couldn't help it. If he thought I could go back to work and never think about how it was between us, he was an idiot.

"This," he leaned over and kissed my breast, "shouldn't be a problem. We'll fit it into our schedules whenever we can."

"I don't want to be 'fit into your schedule.' I want to be..." I was going to say everything to you, but he stopped me.

"My wife?" He shook his head. "Not possible."

Quick as a cat, I straddled him. "Why isn't it possible?"

"It just

"I'm not good enough for you, is that it?"

He grabbed my arms. "Where did that stupid idea come from? As it happens, you're far too good for me. You're beautiful and intelligent…" He shook his head. "I tried to let you go. I couldn't do it."

"I am not going to let you up until you tell me why we can't marry."

Feeling very audacious, I leaned over and licked him. He was still sticky from his cum and he tasted salty and sweet. In response to my onslaught, his muscles clenched.

He could over power me in a minute and throw me off, we both knew that.

"I won't die and live you a widow."

It was so far from what I expected him to say that I sat up and stared at him. "What do you mean, you won't die and leave me a widow?"

"Just what I said."

I was going to drag the truth out of him if I had to sit on him all night. "I appreciate the thought, but why should it be set in stone that you'll die first? I might catch some horrible disease…"

He grabbed my arms. "Don't say that. I couldn't bear to see you suffer."

"Well, I'm suffering now, trying to figure you out. I always had the feeling you were hiding something, not only from me but from your family. What is it, Alex? Are you ill?"

"No," he said, "not yet."

That set my heart beating in quick time. "What do you mean not yet?"

He just looked at me. I could see I wasn't going to get it out of him. Suddenly an idea clicked in my brain. His father. His father had died at the age of forty-nine and left his family destitute.

"You have the same thing your father had."

"Sudden death syndrome. Lovely name, eh? Jane assures me that as long as I take my medication faithfully, I have a seventy percent chance of living a long and productive life. Those aren't good enough odds for me. If we had children…"

I wanted to slap him upside the head. "Do you love me, Alex?"

"Damn it to hell. What has love got to do with it?"

"I'll take that as a yes. Love has everything to do with it. If you love me and I'm willing to take that risk with you, then what's the problem?"

"The problem is I refuse to leave you devastated like my mother was."

"So what was your grand plan? That we just go on having sex together? What if something happened and I got pregnant? Condoms break, birth control pills fail. How about this? I become pregnant, we aren't married and you die? How does that sound? Really peachy, huh?"

"You're being ridiculous."

"No, I'm being realistic, that quality that you're so enamored of." I climbed off of him and stood by the bed. "I always thought you Cameron brothers were the most down to earth, realistic men I'd ever seen. Now I see I was wrong, at least about you. You're trying to play God, Alex. God won't like it. And neither do I." I went into the bathroom and shrugged into a robe. I damped down every objection I had to shutting Alex out of my life and came out of the bathroom, still in full spate. He'd started to dress and had his boxers on. I ignored his beautiful body and kept at it. "I can't go on seeing you every day, loving you the way I do and knowing there is nothing in the future for us but an occasional toss in the hay. I won't be in tomorrow. I'm going back to the coffee shop, if Bob will have me. You can see yourself out."

I went out to my kitchen and starting banging pots around. I wasn't going to cook anything, but the clanging sound made me feel better.

Alex came out of the room fully dressed except for his flapping shirt sleeves. He'd gathered up his cuff links and held them in his hand. He stepped up into the raised floor that delineated the kitchen. "Susan…you can't mean it."

"I do mean it. I'm through, Alex. I love you and I'm through. There. I've said everything there is to say."

"And quite a bit more," he murmured.

"Just…leave, Alex."

He turned his back to me, stepped down off the kitchen floor and went out the door. It was over. I'd never see him again.

The next day was Sunday. My cell phone started ringing while I was still in bed. Alex's name came up on the screen. I clicked the phone off and went in for a shower.

Feeling like a complete ass, I called Bob. He said he'd be glad to have me back and I could start tomorrow. That off my list, I was restless. It felt odd to dress in jeans and know that there was nothing really to do that day. In the first throes of my infatuation for Alex, I'd bought that book by Immanuel Kant. I tried to concentrate on the words, but it wasn't exactly gripping reading. My cell phone rang continuously. I finally turned it off.

A knock sounded at the door. Damn it all. I'd have to kick Alex out of my apartment again.

But when I opened the door, it was Betsy standing there.

"I tried to call you, but the calls all went to voice mail."

I hugged her so hard. I couldn't believe she'd come to see me before leaving on her honeymoon. She looked wonderful in her going away outfit, a lovely taupe dress and a glitzy scarf in rust and black. "I didn't want to leave without telling you how much I appreciated you having the bachelor party here. Everyone said they had a great time. I had a great time, too…I think."

"Come in, come in, and sit for a minute."

She shook her head. "I can't stay. Sam was a little upset with me when I told him I wanted to stop here. I just wanted to say thank you, and I'll miss you. I don't think we have cell reception out there, but maybe I can write…if I remember how," she said smiling.

"Do whatever you can to keep in touch."

"I will. Did you get things straightened out with the gorgeous Alex?"

"All straightened out," I said, not wanting to intrude on her happiness. And it wasn't a lie. I did have things straightened out with Alex. "Betsy, take care of yourself."

She flashed a smile at me. "Oh, I'm going to take care of myself all right. Susan, I just found out this morning. I'm having a baby."

"Oh, Betsy." I hugged her again. "Congratulations. I guess this must have happened before the wedding night."

"Afraid so. Sam is ecstatic. He wanted to start a family right away, even if we are going off to live in a hole in the desert."

"I'm very happy for you. Tell Sam congratulations."

"I will," she said, and then she kissed my cheek and left.

I closed the door, my heart in my throat. Here was Betsy, going off to live in the weirdest, hottest, most uncivilized place on the planet and already pregnant. Talk about brave.

And here was I skulking around my apartment, obsessing about a man who was afraid to take a chance on life. I turned my cell phone on and called Alex.

"Where are you?" I pretty much knew where he was. If we weren't working, he tried to spend Sundays at the family home.

"I'm here at Mother's."

"I need to come and see you. Can you give me a few moments of your precious time?" I supposed that being snippy with Alex wasn't the thing to do, but I couldn't help it.

"I can spare you a minute or two," he drawled.

I pulled up in the circular driveway. Oh, swell, There was Justin's SUV, Hunter's Jaguar, and Lynne's sporty muscle car. And of course Alex's Jeep. It was hail, hail, the gang's all here. I should have waited. Nuts to that. I was going to have it out with him one more time.

He met me in the door and escorted me past the entire family seated in the living room. We went into the library and Alex shut the door. He leaned back against it and folded his arms. "Well?"

I knew it wouldn't be easy to stick to my resolve, especially after we'd just run the gauntlet of his family's lively, curious eyes.

"Betsy is having a baby."

"Good for her," Alex said. He straightened away from the door and started toward me with a look in his eye that made it difficult for me to keep my train of thought.

"She's going to live in Cobber Pedy. Ever heard of it?"

He came closer. "Actually, I have. Opal mine in the desert, I believe."

"With temperatures averaging over a hundred degrees. Hardly any amenities."

He was so close I could see the deep blueness of his eyes.

"She's taking a terrible chance.'"

"That's her choice," he said, not moving just…looking at me.

I pounced. "Exactly. That's her choice. And it's my choice to take a chance on a life with you. Not your choice. Mine."

"I do see the logic in what you're saying."

"Being the logical man that you are, I thought you would."

His arms came around me and he pulled me in to him. "I tried to call you this morning."

"I know. I didn't feel like talking to you…this morning."

"I have something I want to say to you."

"Well? I'm here now and I'm listening." If this was going to be another plea for me to come and work for him, I would have to walk away. And this time, there would be no going back.

He pulled me in until we were nose to nose. I hated it when he did this. He only had to be a hairsbreadth away and I got that signal from my body that this was my mate and I should be mating.

"If you hadn't come to me, I was going to come to you."

Still suspicious, I said, "And say what?"

"I wanted to ask…if you would marry me." He reached in his pocket and brought out a small case. He flipped it open to display a gorgeous ruby ring. "This belonged to my mother. If you'd rather have a traditional diamond…"

"No," I said, knowing that never in my life had I seen anything so beautiful. It was an old-fashioned marquise cut ruby set in a border of diamonds.

"I remembered that you look good in red." He slipped it on my finger. It fit perfectly. "I was right. You do look good in red." His eyes sparkled with pleasure at my delight in having it. I kissed him long and deep. When I felt him walk me backward, knowing he was going to take me down on the couch and do more to seal our engagement than kiss me, the door opened and all the members of the Cameron clan poured in, clapping. Quickly, I pushed Alex away and tried to look like I hadn't been thinking of doing unspeakable things on that bronze leather couch.

    Lynne was first. She whispered in my ear, "I told Alex it was time to pee or get off the pot." Justin came and kissed me on the cheek and then introduced me to his wife Anne. I was right about her. She looked utterly serene with baby Josh in her arms. Natalie, Anne's sister came and said shyly, "Welcome to the family." Hunter's little girl Madeline toddled around the room, finding and grabbing her daddy's leg. Liz came and kissed me. "You're a wonderful addition to this family," she said warmly. I knew that she meant it.

    Amelia had waited until her brood had given me their congratulations before she stepped forward. "I've been waiting for this day a long time. I thought that boy would never come to his senses. Thank you for not giving up on him. He's not an easy man. But he's a good man and he's like his father. He'll love you till the day he dies."

I wondered if she knew what had been bothering Alex. I thought perhaps she didn't. No need for her to know, really.

We decided to get married between Christmas and New Year's. No reason to wait. I only had my parents... and the Cameron family preferred to keep their weddings private.

I found a dress, a simple gown in white lace with cap sleeves, a sweetheart neckline and a flared overskirt. Lynne agreed to be my maid of honor and we found a lovely blue dress in a similar style for her.

Justin played the guitar for Lynne and me to walk down each side of the double staircase in the Cameron mansion. Inside the sitting room, a fire roared in the fireplace while I took my place beside Alex in front of the clergyman. Alex looked long and lean in his black tux. Justin stood next to him, looking every bit as beautiful with his blond hair and easy body.

Alex's dark eyes flashed over me and they were full of admiration...and promise.

We vowed to love each other in sickness and in health. I kept my gaze steady on him when we said these words. Then it was time for Alex to slip the simple gold ring on my finger and say the same words that men and women have been saying to each other for hundreds of years, with this ring I thee wed. And we kissed. We were husband and wife.

Amelia planned a wonderful sit down dinner, but I was too nervous to eat very much. Justin gave the toast, something along the lines of "it took you forever brother, but here you are with the one woman in the world who can put up with you."

When the dinner was over, and we'd said our goodbyes to everyone, Alex grabbed my hand. I picked up my skirt and we raced up the stairs like a couple of kids.

We entered his bedroom where our traveling clothes had been laid out. He turned me around and discovered a corset looking affair with lacing and a tie. He gave a heartfelt groan. I laughed. "It's just for show." I drew down a zipper at the side of the dress. I said, "I'll do this. You get busy on those cuff links."

"I thought you'd want to do them."

"Takes too much time. I want to get on that plane to the Caribbean," I said.

"And she says I have no romance."

"I'll show you lots of romance when we get to a place where it's warm and we can get naked."

At that, he began to undress quickly, all the while keeping one eye out to enjoy the sight of my dress coming down and me standing in nothing but a thong and my white thigh high stockings.

"I can't even touch you?"

"Sorry. No." I knew what would happen if he touched me. We'd fall together on that huge bed of his and we'd never make it to the Caribbean.

"I don't like being married already," he grumbled.

I would have felt sorry for him but I had the antidote. "Didn't you say this place on St. John's of Hunter's was so private we could walk around without any clothes on?"

"Good point." He went to work on his formal gear and was out of it almost as quickly as I was dressed in shorts and a flowery top. Now I was looking at him, long, lean with an erection poking his boxers. With great glee, he said, "No touching."

"Such a vindictive man." He dressed, we grabbed coats and suitcases and went out the door. Down at the bottom of the stairs the family waited to tell us goodbye. "Oh, Alex, just a minute." I ran back into my room and picked up my bridal bouquet. The top stairs landing was a marvelous place to do the traditional bridal toss. I took aim and threw it deliberately at Lynne. She stepped aside, and my bouquet went plop on the floor. Lynne shot me a dark look as if I deserved it. Puzzled, I turned to Alex. He just shook his head. "Don't ask." Amelia stepped out from the back of the family grouping and took Lynne by the arm into the study while the others told us goodbye and gave us hugs.

I wondered what was going on with Lynne. Alex didn't seem to want to discuss it, and even though I was his wife now, that didn't mean I had the right to pry. Sitting beside me in the plane, he gave me a deep probing kiss, and I forgot about Lynne, my body tingling in anticipation for what was to come.

It was night when we reached the villa. The house sat tucked back into a hill with banana trees, palm trees and greenery all around. There wasn't another house in sight. We dumped our suitcases in the bedroom and went out to the living room, all white and island flavored with wildly flowered upholstered seats and backs in turquoise, yellow and red on wicker furniture. Alex said, "There's supposed to be champagne chilling."

He found the lovely bottle wrapped in gold and poured out two glasses. We touched the delicate flutes and drank. He set his glass down deliberately. "I remember someone…oh, yes, it was my wife…saying something about walking around without any clothes on."

His wife. How lovely. I was his wife. "Liz and Anne were telling me about it when they were helping me get dressed."

"Well?"

If he thought I wasn't going to rise to the challenge, he didn't know me as well as he thought he did. I pulled my top over my head, stripped off my bra, stepped out of my shorts and thong. Then I took the champagne flute and never taking my eyes off him, I dribbled some of the cold liquid over my breasts. Then I turned my back on him and went out into the night to stretch out on the cushioned lounger in the lanai. In two seconds he came to me, stripped of his clothes, as nude as I was.

The night was magical, the stars so close and bright, the insects chirping their mating rhapsodies. In the distance, the ocean rose and fell in sighing waves.

"It's beautiful here," I said, raising my glass to him.

"Very beautiful," he said, his eyes on me.

I wanted him so much I ached. I thought he was going to lie beside me, but instead, he came over me and settled on his knees, straddling me. Still holding his glass, he leaned over and licked me where I'd poured the champagne. "Um. Tasty. I think I'd like some more." He poured his champagne on my abdomen to pool in my navel. I gasped at the coldness of it, contrasted with the heat around me. He lapped the tiny bit of liquid out of my navel. When he relaxed back, I took his hand with the glass and poured champagne on his tip. Then I leaned over and licked him all around. When I flicked my tongue over him, he grabbed me and pushed me back. "No more. I need to be inside you."

"How lovely. That's exactly what I want." By now, I was throbbing with sexual hunger.

He set the champagne glass down on the concrete floor. Then he hesitated. "Shall I go get a condom?"

"No," I said, feeling as if I were dying. I guided him to the place where he belonged. When he was inside me, so lovely, so full, I cried out because I had needed this for so long, Alex inside me with nothing between us. I came almost instantly, throbbing around him. He arched back, trying to hold onto his pleasure. We found our rhythm and as I had orgasm after orgasm, he came with me.

Afterwards, he lay beside me, running a questing finger over the tip of my sensitive breast, my abdomen, my navel. "Shower?" he said.

"Not yet. I was thinking about the pool." The house had its own private pool and the water shimmered in the starlight. "I don't want to go inside, it's so lovely out here."

"Very lovely," he said, cupping my breast in one hand. I was astounded to feel the heat, the need rising in me again.

"Alex."

"Yes?" He sounded so innocent.

"Unless you have recovered, you need to stop doing that."

"Not quite recovered, love, but no matter." His hand wandered lower to my mound. "I have other ways of satisfying you."

His fingers slid inside me and I convulsed immediately. I half rose up with the force of it. His dark eyes watching me, his hand still inside me, he moved on top of me. "You are…mine," he said and slid into me. "I'll love you all my life." I couldn't believe there was anything left of me. But Alex found it. We shattered together. For me there was no more dancing in the dark. I was complete.

We spent a whole lovely week, swimming in the pool, making love under the stars. I hated to think of going back, but I knew Alex was starting to feel the need to return and pull his weight with his brothers.

On the plane ride to wintery Rochester, I said, "Alex.

"Yes, my love?"

"You'll have to hire a new assistant."

He looked at me blankly. "Why?"

"Well, I just thought…if I became pregnant…"

"We'll cross that bridge when we come to it. Right now, I'm not going to lose the best assistant I've ever had just because I happen to be married to her."

It thrilled me to think he really didn't want to replace me. "But if I have a baby…"

"We'll bring the little bugger to work with us. He…or she…can learn the business from the ground up."

"You can't be serious."

"I'm dead serious. Susan, you know you love working. And I love having you work with me. The company needs you. I need you. As far as nursing the baby and changing diapers in the office, about that part I don't know. You probably wouldn't want to do that. Maybe you'd take a half year's leave. I don't have all the answers. We'll just make it up as we go along."

I'd always known Alex was a wonderful man. And he'd just proven how right I was about him. My pirate man, Mr. Regular Black had just handed me the world. "Yes," I said, thinking if I were any happier, I wouldn't need this plane to fly. "We'll make it up as we go along."

Thank you for reading the third book in the Cameron Family Saga. I hope you enjoyed it. Please write a review. It would be appreciated.

About the author:

Shirley Larson (also known as Shirley Hart) read her first romance several years ago. She fell in love with the romance genre. Now she has written over thirty romances. She loves every minute of spinning her tales of romance (well, almost every minute) and she hopes her readers enjoy reading them. You can write to her at slarson1943@cfl.rr.com

Books by Shirley Larson

All books available at Amazon and Kindle.

The Cameron Family Saga

Wanting Hunter	Book 1
Wooing Justin	Book 2
Winning Alex	Book 3
A Cowboy for Lynn	Book 4

Other books available from Amazon and Kindle

Branded by Passion

Smokin' Hot Cowboy

I'll Never Say I Love You/ available in print only

Shirley Larson

Can't Get You Out Of My Mind is a sequel to the above book.

The Secret of Jamie's Summer

Historical Romance

Deception by Moonlight

Forbidden Love, Forever Love

In ebook only

That Black Stallion

A Cowboy is Forever

The Medieval Knight a Time Travel Romance

This Love will go on

Can't Get You Out of My Mind is a sequel to the above book